New Wealth

Commercialization of Science and Technology for Business and Economic Development

GEORGE KOZMETSKY,
FREDERICK WILLIAMS, AND
VICTORIA WILLIAMS

Westport, Connecticut
London

Library of Congress Cataloging-in-Publication Data

Kozmetsky, George.
  New wealth : commercialization of science and technology for business and economic
development / George Kozmetsky, Frederick Williams, and Victoria Williams.
     p. cm.
  Includes bibliographical references and index.
  ISBN 1–56720–631–X
     1. Technology—Economic aspects—United States.   2. Technology—Economic
aspects—Caribbean Area.   3. Science and state—United States.   4. Science and state—
caribbean Area.   5. Industrial promotion—United States.   6. Industrial promotion—
caribbean Area.   I. Williams, Frederick, 1933–   II. Williams, Victoria.   III. Title.
HC110.T4K69 2004
338′.064′0973—dc22   2004018596

British Library Cataloguing in Publication Data is available.

Library of Congress Catalog Card Number 2004018596
ISBN: 1–56720–631–X

First published in 2004

Praeger Publishers, 88 Post Road West, Westport, CT 06881
An imprint of Greenwood Publishing Group, Inc.
www.praeger.com

Printed in the United States of America

The paper used in this book complies with the
Permanent Paper Standard issued by the National
Information Standards Organization (Z39.48–1984).

10   9   8   7   6   5   4   3   2   1

Dedicated to the memory of
Thomas Jefferson
third U.S. president
author, scholar, R&D proponent
Renaissance man

Contents

Preface

We wrote *New Wealth: Commercialization of Science and Technology for Business and Economic Development* to be invaluable for anyone who wants to create wealth, including

- entrepreneurs in quest for a larger picture of opportunities in the commercialization of science and technology;
- investors wanting to know the changing opportunities for wealth creation;
- citizen and government leaders seeking strategies for economic development;
- professionals in developmental agencies, ministries, or corporations planning their policies and economic-development programs;
- academic specialists in economic development who are researching and theorizing about economic development in the twenty-first century.

Rarely in our quarter century of projects and research in business and economic development have we found leaders, politicians, planners, entrepreneurs, or just everyday people who did not dream about advancing economically their locality, region, nation, or even themselves by uses of science and technology. Although scientific concepts can be too general or abstract to be of immediate commercial value, or particular technologies too specific to envisage as a means for community or national economic development, together they are a basis for the next generation of the new prosperity. We have seen this in our experiences ranging across the political spectrum from capitalists to communists as well as among those who express no knowledge, interest, or attitudes about the relations of the commercial to the cultural or political.

At the same time, we have also observed and concluded that there are specific strategies for creating wealth in our age of science and technology that are the core of the present book. We have concluded from so very many success stories (including some not-so-successful ones) that collaboration among business, government, entrepreneurial, and academic partners—all focusing to leverage local resources to compete in the global marketplace—is a most powerful strategy for twenty-first-century business creation, and also, therefore, for economic development.

This collaborative success strategy of "thinking globally and acting locally," along with supportive activities such as enterprise centers, business technology incubators, advanced research methods, entrepreneurship training, and use of networks for resource sharing is a modern success model we call the *technopolis paradigm* (chapter 8). Because a maturing technopolis evolves as an integral component of a city, state, or larger sociopolitical unit, it promotes attention to a political economy that supports sustainability and quality of life.

May *New Wealth* serve us all well.

George Kozmetsky
Frederick Williams
Victoria Williams

PART I

Science and Technology as the New Prosperity

CHAPTER 1

Technology as a Wealth Concept

There has never been a more opportune time than in our age of burgeoning science and technology for the creation of new prosperity. For most of history, the sources of wealth depended upon the extraction of value from nature, as in hunting, fishing, farming, or mining, which the renowned economist Daniel Bell[1] called the *pre-industrial age*; later, sources of wealth depended upon adding value through processing or fabricating goods from these natural resources, which, by contrast, he called the *industrial age*; and still later, with the coming of our *post-industrial age*, sources of wealth depended upon knowledge, information, or know-how for enhancing the foregoing.

CLAIMING THE NEW PROSPERITY

Today, we talk of the *commercialization of science and technology,* which is the basis for vast opportunities in the creation of new products and services or the enhancement of existing ones. But science and technology are not just for the already affluent; they can offer so many fresh opportunities for small or very traditional underperforming economies to be transformed into a new, shared, and sustained prosperity—and, most important, for enhancement in the quality of everyday life. Science and technology are sustainable sources of wealth. Business and development opportunities are there for the claiming if only entrepreneurs, investors, and political leaders will pursue them.

FAILURE OF GLOBAL ECONOMIC POLICY MAKING

Unfortunately, we cannot look to substantial progress in global cooperation regarding sustainable economic development. The United Nations' Earth Summit II, held during August 2002 in Johannesburg, South Africa, fell into discord as small, poorer nations castigated the major wealthy nations for the impositions of globalization and an unwillingness to sign treaties agreeing to deadlines on such policies as renewable energy sources (more below).

BBC dispatches from the summit provide a glimpse and flavor of the proceedings—for example, in Secretary-General Kofi Annan's charge to global big businesses:

Raising the use of renewable energy is still unresolved. Some of the world's most powerful business leaders have been told they must invest in developing countries for the mutual benefit of rich and poor. The call at the World Development Summit came from United Nations Secretary-General Kofi Annan, who said that sustainable business investment was essential if poor countries were to escape poverty. "Today there is a growing recognition all around that lasting and effective answers can only be found if business joins in partnership and works with others," he said in Johannesburg. "We're close to the wire, we're on the last lap." Nitin Desai, summit secretary-general, added that ". . . It is only by mobilizing the corporate sector that we can make significant progress." He said that since the first Earth summit ten years ago, business leaders had realized that if they wanted to survive, in a sometimes hostile global economy, they had to respond to social and environmental challenges. Business leaders called for more dialogue between companies and environmental campaigners at the summit, challenging the view that they were enemies of the green movement. Many countries want to set a deadline for improved water supplies. Shell Oil Chairman Phil Watts urged firms not to take bribes and to work in closer partnership with local firms in developing countries. However, the BBC's Tim Hirsch in Johannesburg says there are disagreements as to whether business activity should be left to voluntary controls or regulated by governments at a global level. As the summit enters its second week, negotiators are racing against time to achieve workable agreements on renewable energy as heads of state arrive on Monday. After a marathon session, delegates said they would reconvene later on Monday to try to resolve the one remaining dispute about energy. Some countries have been pushing for 10% of the world's power to come from renewable sources by 2010. But not everyone backs that deadline, and there is also debate about exactly how renewable energy should be defined. "We're close to the wire, we're on the last lap," Conference Secretary-General Nitin Desai told Reuters news agency late on Sunday night. "Countries are finding common ground." BBC correspondents say a major hurdle remains targets on the use of clean energy such as wind and solar power and on the increase of the provision of decent sanitation for the poor. This document can be found at: http://www.earthsummit2.org.

By the conclusion of Summit II, the major motions failed, as large countries with large investments in energy resources were not about to have their agendas set by small countries who, after all, had few resources to commit. So, at the outset of this volume, we must acknowledge that global cooperation for economic development has a long way to go.

HOW DO WE PROCEED? BACKGROUND AND STRATEGIES, PLAN OF THE VOLUME

From our many years of research and experience concentrating upon science and technology as an economic resource, coupled with an abundance of literature from others, we have developed an overall five-part structure for *New Wealth* that begins with a historical and philosophical background.

Part I, "Science and Technology as the New Prosperity," comprises four chapters. In chapter 1, we explain this new-wealth concept and try to emphasize its importance in the current global economy. In chapter 2, we review how Adam Smith's philosophy, as expressed in his *Wealth of Nations,* is now manifested in our times as opportunities offered for individual and corporate prosperity through the commercialization of science and technology in free markets, and how advances in the same, if properly pursued and their social ramifications directed toward positive ends, are the path to shared prosperity—all eventually for the public good. The key to success strategies is the technology-based enterprise, the characteristics of which are the topic of chapter 3. These new enterprises, especially in today's world, are best "thought globally while developed locally," as described in chapter 4.

Part II, "Managing in Fast Company," in eight chapters, stresses how an economy based on science and technology must keep pace with perpetual change, including technology transfer, manufacturing, and marketing. To compete, businesses must accelerate their component operations to meet this pace of change. So too must government and development agencies. As discussed in chapter 5, winners are accelerating their managerial strategies, including a client-customer gratification strategy that Raymond Yeh and his colleagues call *Zero Time.* Much of the acceleration of business operations today depends upon combinations of computing and telecommunications, and networks in particular. Our understanding and improvement of networks linking suppliers, customer, investors, and partners are much enhanced today by advances in the theory of complex networks (chapter 6). We must learn to manage in *fast company* using technology to teach technology, as described in chapter 7. Critical in contemporary technology-based economic development is the integration of the commercial entity through the goal of shared socioeconomic progress with the community, a topic we develop in chapter 8 as constructing the *technopolis*. Commercialization of science and technology is an information-intensive process that we describe in more detail in discussions of the adoption of innovations and technology transfer in chapters 9 and 10, respectively. Industrial parks, business incubators, and the new so-called enterprise centers are new catalytic facilities to support business development (chapters 11 and 12), especially with the rapid pace of growth in science and technology.

Part III, "Advances in Management Science," offers two chapters on powerful research tools for managers. Growing demands for planning and evaluation have placed a new emphasis upon the need for sophisticated tools for applied research (chapter 13). Added to these are much improved, easily used methods for decision science and risk analysis, the topics of chapter 14.

Part IV, "Revitalizations," includes five wide-ranging, dynamic examples of "take-charge" economics, ranging as wide as how Austin, Texas, a capital and college town, reinvented itself as a technology center (chapter 15); how a binational U.S.-Mexican program has sparked development along their joint borderlands (chapter 16); how Caribbean nations can diversify from tourism economies, retaining their pristine environments and aiming for a "prosperity in paradise" (chapter 17); how Venezuelans seek to cross-invest oil profits and economically diversify in their land-rich State of Anzoátegui (chapter 18); and, finally, how Cuba, in a view not often seen in the North American press, identified and developed biotechnology as a source of wealth and added to it a noteworthy emphasis upon development of human resources through education and health services (chapter 19).

Concluding, Part V, "Prosperity Sharing," is a single chapter that, while respecting and advocating free enterprise and capitalism, tries to address its weakness in sharing the wealth. Can we have capitalism with a conscience?

All withstanding, we are within an age not only opportune for the formation of personal and social financial success from the commercialization of science and technology, but one in which informed and inspired individual entrepreneurs, government ministers, or economic development officers can create and share the new wealth for the enhancement of quality of life for their city, state, region, or nation. Moreover, science and technology can contribute directly to quality of life through such applications as health care and education. This, again, is what we mean by "Science and Technology as the New Prosperity," and achieving it is what this book is all about.

NOTE

1. Daniel Bell, *The Coming of Post-Industrial Society* (New York: Basic Books, 1976).

CHAPTER 2

Today's Wealth of Nations

The year 1776, a noteworthy American milestone, was also the year of publication of Scottish professor Adam Smith's *The Wealth of Nations*, the first great book on modern economics and the foundation of thought on free enterprise. Wealth, of course, can take on a variety of forms, with most personal forms signifying ownership or command over goods, services, or access to money or credit reflecting the value of the same. In this chapter, we develop a large-scale picture of global wealth as a basis to contrast nations as they appear to take advantage or have fallen behind in opportunities for economic advancement and quality of life.

GROSS DOMESTIC PRODUCT

The economic concept of GDP, or gross domestic product—the total value of goods and services produced over a year—is an accepted measure. In the present book, unless we state otherwise, GDP for international comparative purposes is given as dollar estimates derived from "purchasing power parity" (PPP) calculations based upon analysis of the dollar value of goods and services, not a conversion from local currencies. Although OECD (Organization for Economic Cooperation and Development) country values are considered reliable, values for developing countries can be only approximations.[1] To facilitate national comparisons relative to population size, GDP per capita (GDP divided by the population size) is often employed. GDP is sometimes divided among economic sectors of agriculture, industry, and service, the latter of which is quite a mix but does include banking, government services, and sometimes tourism services, to name a few.

Selected main figures from the 2001 CIA *Factbook* analysis appear in table 2.1.

GDP NATIONAL COMPARISONS

The world's nations show stark contrast between rich and poor. The *Factbook* represents 267 nations (plus small miscellaneous dependent areas) with a total (GDP sum) gross world product (GWP) of $43.66 trillion. About half ($21 trillion) of this total represents the wealthy so-called Group of 8 (G8), six of which—the United States, Japan, the United Kingdom, Italy, Germany, and Russia—began meeting in 1975 to negotiate certain international economic issues, with Russia recently joining as a member. Roughly half of the G8 GDP sum is due to the United States

Table 2.1
Selected World Data from the 2001 *CIA Factbook*

DEMOGRAPHY

Population estimate	**23,916,810**
Infant mortality	**25.37/1,000**
Life expectancy	**73.31 years**
Literacy	**91.10%**

ECONOMY

GDP (2000 estimate)	**$146.2 billion**
GDP per capita	**$6,200**
Labor Force	**9.9 million**
In agriculture	**13%**
In industry	**23%**
In services	**64%**

LAND USE (1993)

Arable	**4%**
Permanent crops	**1%**
Pastures	**20%**
Forests	**34%**
Other	**41%**

Figure 2.1
Division of Gross World Product. $43.66 trillion sum of GDPs among the United States, other G8 nations, and remaining nations, including China.

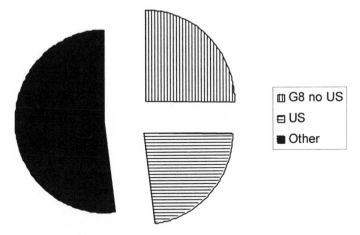

▥	G8 no US
▤	US
▮	Other

($9.963 trillion). Of the others, China accounts for $4.5 trillion, leaving average countries at less than $10 billion in average GDP. Figure 2.1 illustrates this division of the gross world product.

As of figures for 2001, China had a GDP of $4.5 trillion, but when this purchasing power is estimated relative to its population (1.3 billion) the GDP per capita ($2,300) puts China among poorer nations in terms of relative wealth per person. But note that over half the $21 trillion of the GWP is contributed by the wealthy G8. Of the G8, the United States, with a GDP of $9.963 trillion, has 23 percent of the GWP. Or, looked at in terms of GWP per capita, the U.S. GDP per capita is about five times that of the world average.

When accounting for population differences (GDP per capita), countries show a stark contrast. Following are some comparative figures from the *Factbook:*

Examples of GDP Per Capita

Afghanistan, $800

Brazil, $6,500

Congo, $1,100

Cuba, $1,700

Denmark, $25,500

Ethiopia, $600

Gaza Strip, $1,000

Israel, $18,900

Kenya, $1,500

Mexico, $9,100

Nigeria, $950

North Korea, $1,000 est.

Norway, $27,700

Saudi Arabia, $10,500

South Korea, $16,000

Vietnam, $1,950

West Bank, $1,500

CONTRASTING WEALTHY AND POOR ECONOMIES

One overriding generalization about wealthy countries with favorable GDPs, or especially GDPs per capita, is that they typically have a market economy coupled with major industrial sectors, and, as with the G8 countries, have reaped the benefits of technology and expand that benefit. China is an interesting example: President Jiang Zemin has led a movement of adapting their central-planned communist economy into an internationally competitive market, one with a major eye toward the adoption of plans for development of science and technology. This was the focus of a major Central Economic Working Conference conducted in November of 2001.[2] At another extreme, most of the poorer countries of the world have sizeable populations living a bare subsistence existence on the land. This contributes to inefficient performance in the agricultural sector with clear evidence of failure in uses of modern crop planning and management—a waste of natural resources.

From the aforementioned analyses, we can identify abundant opportunities for new wealth creation, both for the individual entrepreneur and the economic-development specialist.

NOTES

1. This is the method used by the U.S. Central Intelligence Agency in their annual *Factbook*, and draws from the UN International Comparison Program (UNICP) and Professors Robert Summers and Alan Heston of the University of Pennsylvania and their colleagues. The *Factbook* can be ordered from the CIA or found at http://www.odci.gov/cia/publications/factbook/.

2. Information on this may be found in the English-language pages of the *People's Daily* on the World Wide Web. This is in contrast to fellow communist Fidel Castro, who continues to condemn the free-market, or neoliberal, economy, although his leaders do acknowledge their need for increased competitiveness and more adoption of technology. In their "special period" after the loss of Russian assistance, Cuba was successful in boosting tourism with the plan to invest profits

in industrial development. Still, the U.S. trade embargo has made it very difficult to expand technology transfer. Reports on this can be found on the World Wide Web and in several of Dr. Castro's books listed in our bibliography. His books and speeches make good reading whether or not you agree with him. Havana, with his direct support and involvement, has been the site of annual economic conferences conducted by the Latin American and Cuban Economics Associations.

CHAPTER 3

Technology-Based Enterprise Creation

Businesses created from science and technology or enhanced by the same have distinguishing characteristics, research into which has occupied the IC^2 (innovation, capital, creativity) Institute for over three decades. We begin this chapter with a discussion of these characteristics, then go on to examine policy and performance implications. We conclude the chapter with summary notes on telecommunication- and computer-based commerce systems *(e-commerce)*.

EIGHT KEY GENERALIZATIONS

Beginning in 1977 and continuing as a major thrust of our work today, research fellows of the IC^2 Institute have concentrated on the specific aspects of technology-based enterprise creation. We began in a cooperative study project with the Conference Board, an independent, nonprofit business research organization,[1] with the initial goal of identifying those variables apparently critical in the creation of businesses where success was based on the commercialization of technologies, application, or both. The board's sole purpose is to promote prosperity and security by assisting in the effective operation and sound development of voluntary, productive enterprises. Its organization consists of more than 4,000 associates and serves 40,000 individuals throughout the world. It does continuing research in the fields of economic conditions, marketing, finance, personnel administration, international activities, public affairs, and antitrust and various related areas. Our research program was the first in the IC^2 series of management-of-change studies.

In the broad view, we saw that technology is both a resource and tool of knowledge and know-how, as well as the new platform for doing business in the age of science and technology. Our research confirmed the following:

1. **Technology as wealth:** We need to understand technology as a type of wealth— one that may often require new concepts for measurement (nowadays, "digital economy," for example). Traditionally, of course, wealth is a means of attaining economic, social, and cultural status for individuals, as well as a way of achieving institutional objectives and ensuring the general welfare of society.

2. **Need for technology policy:** Technology innovation is a prime factor in stimulating productive capacity and ensuring healthy competitive international trade. Thus far, few, if any, nations have formulated such critical policies.

3. **Market interaction:** Each nation's technological needs are linked with other nations' commercial needs. In no case is one market wholly insulated from what happens to other markets.

4. **Need for managerial know-how:** All nations—industrialized or emerging or less developed—need effective technological management and entrepreneurial training at all levels in both the private and public sectors and in operations.

5. **Technology transfer:** Technology commercialization is not a simple transfer of a product or service; it is a process that has application to existing means of design, production, distribution, and maintenance as well as to developing commercial applications new to the world.

6. **Fast-company design:** Technologies change so rapidly and market appetite so quickly that companies specializing in science and technology commercialization have no alternative except to match or exceed the pace of change; they must become *fast companies,* and it is a mark of the times.

7. **New management strategies:** Entrepreneurs and researchers can develop road maps for technologies that are key variables for venture creation.

8. **Enhanced applied research:** The foregoing requires a new emphasis upon applied research tools, including decision science and risk analysis, to distinguish them from more traditional methods for theoretical or more traditional "basic" research, so to speak.

POLICY IMPLICATIONS

Public policy can have an influence on each of the above components and thus on the conditions under which the promotion of technological activities depends. Following are key points:

- **New alliances:** A wide range of public policies and programs, and of new economic development alliances, particularly at the local and state levels, has emerged in the United States that relate to each of these factors and that seek to influence the entrepreneurial process. Many of these may be appropriate or modified to other infrastructure areas.

- **Indigenous company growth:** Local company development has become an important long-term economic development strategy across the world for several reasons.

- **Harnessing local entrepreneurial talent:** It is so often local talent and resources and the associated commitment that build companies, which, in turn, create jobs and add economic value to a region and community. Locally based strategies can help keep homegrown talent and profits within the community to become models for others. They encourage economic diversification and technological innovation by seeking to create a climate that rewards productivity and innovation.

- **Building the talent pool:** Policies seeking to influence conditions promoting the local talent pool should include enhancements to quality of life, education, human services, and cultural and recreational attractions; improvements to the local infrastructure; recognition of successful role models; and development of a culture conducive to creativity and innovation.

- **R&D payoff:** Priority should be given to policies seeking to influence the conditions affecting the development of technology; these include state- and federal-government funding programs for R&D; application of more effective, "market-pull" technology transfer mechanisms within the R&D performers; establishment of industrial and science parks and business incubators; creation of R&D consortia; and improvements in intellectual-property policies to encourage a sense of ownership for the developers of technological innovations.

- **Capital:** Policies seeking to influence the conditions affecting the availability of capital include the establishment of computerized business-angel networks, the creation of government programs to assist the start-up of new technology ventures (such as the Small Business Innovation Research Program), tax advantages for those investing in new companies (such as R&D tax credits and capital-gains modifications), the organization of small-business investment corporations, and the creation of state venture-capital funds.

- **Technical know-how:** Policies seeking to influence the initial conditions affecting the availability of business and technical know-how include the establishment of new business incubators; the availability of educational programs for business-training assistance; the development of technical support and assistance programs; and the development of organized networks of experienced businesspeople, local advisors, and professional associations and support groups.

CHANGES IN PERFORMANCE

Pioneering

All institutions seeking economic development in our rapidly expanding era of new science and technology must pioneer in developing the knowledge base as well as centers for the performance of creating ventures in communities, regions, nations, and around the world. The technologies of our era, as well as the newer digital-knowledge economy, will continue to transform the role and scope of universities, technological industries, laboratories, and government in venture creation.

Upgraded Norms

The norm of providing world-class products or services at the best price and highest quality is insufficient. Computing and communication will continue to shrink time and space. The new generation of customers will come to expect instant gratification. Creating ventures that can respond with instant gratification in Zero Time is the charge to our universities. Zero Time creation of ventures is a new requirement for university research and instruction. It will require the extension of disciplines as well as the generation of newer transdisciplines for (1) customer satisfaction and gratification, (2) knowledge transformation into value, (3) lifelong education and training for all skill levels in less than normal degree-granting time intervals, (4) adaptation in Zero Time of advanced processes to generate and distribute newer products and services, and (5) timely removal of barriers for instant adaptation of the enterprise for the global/local markets.

Intellectual Wealth

As compared with traditional sources of wealth such as those extracted from nature (e.g., oil and mining), developed with nature (agriculture), or developed from manufacturing and services, in our contemporary era, intellectual capital as embedded in science and technology is an enormous source of wealth—and most striking of all, distinctively human.

TECHNICAL CHALLENGES OF LARGE-SCALE ENTRY INTO E-COMMERCE

There is so much literature on the operations and the ins and outs of e-commerce that we will not go into such details here. Instead, we will offer notes on the technological challenge of large-scale entry into the business.[2] We phrase the points as questions facing the technology manager.

Business-to-Consumer (B2C) Applications

1. Given the demographics of the audience using the Internet, do consumers have the hardware and software compatible with the features and functions of the company Web site to enable them to use it? This must be monitored and taken advantage of as technology improves.

2. What is the competition on the Internet? What is the competition's demographic footprint, their Internet site features, their frequency of updating their presence on the Internet? What is the timing of lead/lag on the Internet, and how can this be measured against competition to assist in sustaining marketability?

3. The cost of creating, maintaining, and administering a major B2C e-commerce business can require $1 million to $5 million in start-up capital. The large-scale company will need to continuously update its Web front as well as supporting databases of consumer information, customer orders, and transaction records.

4. Internet sites do not become known by themselves alone; they must be promoted by complementary media campaigns. Knowing demographic market and reach are essential. Required are multimedia campaigns (print, radio, TV, etc.) in addition to the firm's Web presence. Some U.S. marketing campaigns range up to $20 million for online "heavy goods" businesses (e.g., automotive)—per quarter.

5. Rapid e-commerce process change occurs as quickly as two weeks, and flexibility, speed, and ability—technological capability—to adapt to change are keys to success.

Business-to-Business (B2B) Applications

1. What are the networking advantages if the business is using the Internet to communicate with outsourcers and to supplement management, marketing, information diffusion, or sales reach? Usage goals must match the objectives of the core business. What are the gains in market share, higher margins, and, of course, return on investment?

2. A "fast corporate" business model requires the ability to monitor, adapt, and redefine its business strategy; the model will be constantly impacted by competition, technology, marketing, and economic factors.

3. Technology (mirrored servers, offsite servers) must be redundant to protect against failure.

4. Scalability requires that technology be adapted to changing market size. Can infrastructure, systems, and human resources handle the changing traffic?

5. Sustainability is critical for maintaining a competitive edge. For example, computer telephony integration: forms of text chat, live chat, and integrated pop-up windows—being able to view and guide the customer on a real-time Web site window. To maintain a competitive edge, a company must be concurrently working on the next level of technology.

6. Web front- and back-end databases require stable infrastructure to ensure continuity of presence on the Internet. There are downtimes, maintenance, and emergency situations.

7. What should be benchmarks and measurements for performance of individuals, teams, departments, and corporations?

8. What are the measures for costs due to lack of performance?

9. How does technology failure (servers, telecom) lead to particular types of business interruptions (lost opportunities, lost sales, etc.)?

10. What are the corresponding remedies?

11. How can a business demand a form of payback (compensation, discounts, enhanced service) due to failure of the technology provider?

IN CONCLUSION

In closing this section on e-commerce and the chapter, we return to underscore our opening point that *technology is both a resource and tool of knowledge and know-how, as well the new platform for doing business in the age of science and technology.*

NOTES

1. The Conference Board is a nonprofit business membership and research organization for senior executives internationally. It produces the *Consumer Confidence Index* and *Leading Economic Indicators.* Contact: The Conference Board Inc., 845 Third Avenue, New York, New York 10022-6679; tel: (212) 759-0900; fax: (212) 980-7014.

2. We are indebted to Ms. Mary Nelson, formerly operations director of the Internet-based U.S. company Carsdirect.com, for an extensive interview on this topic.

CHAPTER 4

Think Globally, Act Locally

The title of this chapter is an axiom of the IC^2 Institute; it is found in most every major speech and paper of George Kozmetsky over 30 years. It is simple and clear, yet complex in its breadth. There are three levels of concern. First, experience often shows that development involving local resources and the galvanization of local leadership is the most apt to be successful and sustaining. Second, however, is that "globally" forces attention to larger markets. Firms wishing to fare well in businesses relating to science and technology have to realize that success will depend upon addressing the burgeoning global markets and also competition for their products and services. Third, finally, is how "globally" conjures up the international-policy arguments about globalization—mainly how what is good policy for the large and rich countries is not necessarily the best for every country, especially those newly developing or changing. The latter is the gist of the current diatribes, marches, and protests against globalization. So "acting locally" can just as well refer to respecting a particular country's interests, or, as much as policymakers seek consistency in global economic practices, they must take the local, individual nation into account. In all, we touch on most all connotations of thinking globally and acting locally in this chapter and will freely move among them, our main point being that the advice found over the years in many Kozmetsky writings and speeches—"Think globally, act locally"—is alive and well.

GLOBALIZATION PROS AND CONS

View from a Small, Very Poor Nation

In his poignant little book *Eyes of the Heart*, Jean-Bertrand Aristide, first democratically elected president of Haiti, opens with an anecdote of a morgue worker interrupted in his task of removing bodies by a man who rises and declares that he is not dead. "Yes, you are. The doctors say that you are dead, so lie down!"[1] The president goes on to describe the plight of this poorest country in the Western Hemisphere in our era of economic globalization. To have any hopes of growth, they, as well as most developing or changing countries, must follow directives of interventional lenders, which are not always to the local advantage.

International Criticism

Effective criticisms are raised about having to succumb to overbearing global capitalistic interests, including from Wall Street, which in the year of this writing suffers from the greatest cases of fiscal corruption in U.S. history. There has been no shortage at international conferences of public displays of protest against the world's rich nations, and especially against the United States. An estimated 10,000 marchers in protest at the conclusion of the UN Earth Summit II, held in Johannesburg, South Africa, in the summer of 2002, declared in signs, songs, and diatribes that globalization, with its control by the rich nations of the world, was a cause of poverty and hopelessness among many small and poor nations.

President Fidel Castro of Cuba, no matter what one's own political values, must be given credit for articulation and publication of the disbenefits of globalization to small countries like his.[2]

Recently, globalization has been seen as high on the lists of terrorist network al Qaeda's complaints about the Western-dominated global economy. Of recent value in understanding the issues has been the publication of and critical reaction to the book *Globalization and Its Discontents*[3] by Joseph E. Stiglitz, Nobel Prize–winning economist and former chief economist of the World Bank. Although the book is more about the World Bank and International Monetary Fund than globalization per se, it shows how even the proponents and administrators of globalization are deep into the fray.

Academic Biases

A focus on local against global is also a recurring debate in how academics look at world change, whether it be in politics, culture, war zones, or economics. Given a particular issue, like ethnic conflict, there is a natural tension between deciding to concentrate research resources on a specific case, area, or region—for example, a political-cultural topic like the

Israeli-Palestinian conflict, or a specific economic one like agricultural subsidies[4]—as against trying to interpret situations or phenomena in a global context. As with most undertakings, scholars must decide how to concentrate their limited funds and time, decisions which are also affected by sponsors or research and projects, as well as the biases of the particular academic field, whether it be economics, political science, international relations, public administration, or area studies, to name a few. In sum, whether an issue is researched, written about, or taught from a local or global view may be as much the bias of the scholar as the priorities emanating from the issue or topic itself.

Expect No End Soon to the Globalization Debate

In sum, "flat out" requirements for uniform monetary policy, trade and tariff practices, and every possible adjustment for market-driven free-enterprise economic practices—mostly as conditions for loans—have caused substantial problems for countries undergoing economic change, whether they be developing Third Worlders or formerly socialist or communist economies moving to a market economy, as with the former Soviet Union. There will always be a strain between what is supposedly best for global economic reform as opposed to local preferences and realities.

ADMONITIONS FOR BUSINESS AND
DEVELOPMENTAL LEADERSHIP

The setting for rethinking technology's role in shaping the global economy can best be described as a lack of consensus on the rules of the game. Of course, there are well-known rules for patents, trading practices, and so forth; but there is no discipline forcing countries to pursue more compatible policies.

Advances in technology—regardless of where they are made or who makes them—will be reflected in national economic structural changes that will compound the problems of macroeconomic change in international trade and payments. This means that leaders, while they are making domestic choices, will need to take into account their impact on other nations' economic structures. For example, Japan has used its technology to make significant inroads into the world's semiconductor markets while maintaining a competitive national market.

The Russian and the Japanese examples make it clear that it is necessary to differentiate international competition from domestic market competition. International competitiveness reflects differences in the ways technology is developed, transferred, and commercialized. The more specific differences lie in the relationships between each national government and its private sectors and the cultural differences that affect how managers measure success in commercializing technology innovations (e.g., return on investments, profits, employment stability, market share, short-term gains, long-term benefits, and relative change in productivity). In the future world economy, these differences can well change the world's economic leadership, which can, in turn, change regional relationships for extended periods of time.

How, then, do we put our arms around the changes, paradoxes, issues, crises, changes, concerns, and problems of today's setting for understanding the role of technology innovation in the growing global economy? Any discussion of the economic future must have a clear notion of how a given society "hangs together"—how its parts are related to one another, and which elements are more susceptible to change than others. These discussions also must take into account the interplays of values, motivations, and resources of differing political and cultural systems. Leadership needs to provide the necessary catalyst that assures a creative environment for change that empowers the clients themselves to translate intentions into realities and sustain them. Beyond international economic institutions with managers who are striving for a more abstract universal global economic reform, we need hands-on leaders and cooperating local associates who do the right things for the specific country. This means thinking globally, but acting nationally and locally.

NOTES

1. Jean-Bertrand Aristide, *Eyes of the Heart: Seeking a Path for the Poor in the Age of Globalization* (Monroe, Maine: Common Courage Press, 2000), p. 9.

2. See, for example, Castro's *Capitalismo Actual* (La Habana, Cuba: Ocean Press, 1999). To Dr. Castro's credit is sponsorship of an annual economic conference on problems of development in the Caribbean and South America. In the four meetings I (FW) attended as a presenter and participant, the president was far more than a titular host; he participated in most major sessions, often offering targeted technical questions prompting lively debate on topics like globalization and issues of neoliberalism (free enterprise). Receiving a standing ovation after prefacing his closing remarks for a day's session by saying, "I'll be brief"—to which he led the laughter—was testimony to this leader's ease and confidence in discussing economic inequities to small countries without getting into political diatribes.

3. Joseph Stiglitz, *Globalization and Its Discontents* (New York: W. W. Norton, 2002); see also subsequent notes on the critiques.

4. Cf. "Farmer on the Dole," *New York Times*, 25 August 2002, the World, p. 10.

PART II

Managing in Fast Company

CHAPTER 5

Fast Companies and Zero Time

As noted throughout this book, and to stress it here, science and technology are not only replenishable resources but are in a state of perpetual change. To seize upon their value requires companies to accelerate their business processes so as to keep pace with change—as with changes in scientific invention, changes in commercialization potential, and speeding up of technology transfer (chapter 10); adapting and accelerating manufacturing strategies; and keeping pace with as well as anticipating changes in the marketplace and marketing processes. We call successful firms in this era *fast companies*. Doing business in this new world of perpetual change means competing with other companies as well as governments and developmental agencies who are speeding up their own operations— or, as we say in this part's title, you are "moving in fast company."

PATENTS AS THE PULSE OF TECHNOLOGICAL CHANGE

United States Patent and Trademark Office

The view from the United States Patent and Trademark Office (USPTO) offers striking facts about the level of scientific invention in this country. As of this writing, the number of patent applications per year has been edging toward 400,000, the increase and importance of which has prompted Congress to mandate streamlining the applications process.

Functions of the United States Patent and Trademark Office

The USPTO is an agency of the U.S. Department of Commerce. The role of the USPTO is to grant patents for the protection of inventions and to register trademarks. It serves the interest of inventors and businesses with respect to their inventions, corporate products, and serves service identifications. It also advises and assists the president of the United States, the secretary of commerce, the bureaus and offices of the Department of Commerce, and other agencies of the government in matters involving all domestic and global aspects of intellectual property. Through the preservation, classification, and dissemination of patent information, the USPTO promotes the industrial and technological progress of the nation and strengthens the economy.

In discharging its patent-related duties, the USPTO examines applications and grants patents on inventions when applicants are entitled to them; it publishes and disseminates patent information, records assignments of patents, maintains search files of U.S. and foreign patents, and maintains a search room for public use in examining issued patents and records. It supplies copies of patents and official records to the public. It provides training to practitioners and their applicants as to requirements of the patent statutes and regulations, and it publishes the "Manual of Patent Examining Procedure" to elucidate these. Similar functions are performed relating to trademarks. By protecting intellectual endeavors and encouraging technological progress, the USPTO seeks to preserve the United States' technological edge, which is key to our current and future competitiveness. The USPTO also disseminates patent and trademark information that promotes an understanding of intellectual-property protection and facilitates the development and sharing of new technologies worldwide.

What Are Patents, Trademarks, Service Marks, and Copyrights?

What Is a Patent? A patent for an invention is the grant of a property right to the inventor, issued by the USPTO. Generally, the term of a new patent is 20 years from the date on which the application for the patent was filed in the United States or, in special cases, from the date an earlier related application was filed, subject to the payment of maintenance fees. U.S. patent grants are effective only within the United States, U.S. territories, and U.S. possessions. Under certain circumstances, patent-term extensions or adjustments may be available.

The right conferred by the patent grant is, in the language of the statute and of the grant itself, "the right to exclude others from making, using, offering for sale, or selling" the invention in the United States or "importing" the invention into the United States. What is granted is not the right to make, use, offer for sale, sell, or import, but the right to exclude others from making, using, offering for sale, selling, or importing the invention. Once a patent is issued, the patentee must enforce the patent without aid from the USPTO.

The Three Types of Patents

1. *Utility patents* may be granted to anyone who invents or discovers any new and useful process, machine, article of manufacture, or composition of matters, or any new useful improvement thereof.
2. *Design patents* may be granted to anyone who invents a new, original, and ornamental design for an article of manufacture.
3. *Plant patents* may be granted to anyone who invents or discovers and asexually reproduces any distinct and new variety of plants.

What Is a Trademark or Service Mark? A trademark is a word, name, symbol, or device that is used in trade with goods to indicate the source of the goods and to distinguish them from the goods of others. A service mark is the same as a trademark except that it identifies and distinguishes the source of a service rather than a product. The terms *trademark* and *mark* are commonly used to refer to both trademarks and service marks. Trademark rights may be used to prevent others from using a confusingly similar mark, but not to prevent others from making the same goods or from selling the same goods or services under a clearly different mark. Trademarks that are used in interstate or foreign commerce may be registered with the USPTO. The registration procedure for trademarks and general information concerning trademarks is described in a separate pamphlet entitled "Basic Facts about Trademarks."

What Is a Copyright? Copyright is a form of protection provided to the authors of "original works of authorship," including literary, dramatic, musical, artistic, and certain other intellectual works, both published and unpublished. The 1976 Copyright Act generally gives the owner of a copyright the exclusive right to reproduce the copyrighted work, to prepare derivative works, to distribute copies or photocopies of the copyrighted work, to perform the copyrighted work publicly, and to display the copyrighted work publicly.

The copyright protects the form of expression rather than the subject matter of the writing. For example, a description of a machine could be copyrighted, but this would only prevent others from copying the description; it would not prevent others from writing a description of their own or from making and using the machine. Copyrights are registered by the Copyright Office of the Library of Congress.

The United States Patent and Trademark Office

Congress established the USPTO to issue patents on behalf of the government. The Patent Office as a distinct bureau dates from 1802, when a separate official in the Department of State, who became known as *superintendent of patents,* was placed in charge of patents. The revision of the patent laws enacted in 1836 reorganized the Patent Office and designated the official in charge as *commissioner of patents*. The Patent Office remained in the Department of State until 1849, when it was transferred to the Department of Interior. In 1925 it was transferred to the Department of Commerce, where it is today. In 1975, the name of the Patent Office was changed to the Patent and Trademark Office.

The USPTO administers the patent laws as they relate to the granting of patents for inventions and performs other duties relating to patents. It examines applications for patents to determine if the applicants are entitled to patents under the law and grants the patents when they are so entitled; publishes issued patents, most patent applications filed on or after November 29, 2000, at 18 months from the earliest filing date, and various publications concerning patents; records assignments of patents; maintains a search room for the use of the public to examine issued patents and records; supplies copies of records and other papers; and the like.

Similar functions are performed with respect to the registration of trademarks. The USPTO has no jurisdiction over questions of infringement and the enforcement of patents, nor over matters relating to the promotion or utilization of patents or inventions.

The head of the USPTO is the undersecretary of commerce for intellectual property and director of the United States Patent and Trademark Office. The director's staff includes the deputy undersecretary of commerce and deputy director of the USPTO, the commissioner for patents, the commissioner for trademarks, and other officials. As head of the office, the director superintends or performs all duties respecting the granting and issuing of patents and the registration of trademarks; exercises general supervision over the entire work of the USPTO; prescribes the rules, subject to the approval of the secretary of commerce, for the conduct of proceedings in the USPTO and for recognition of attorneys and agents; decides various questions brought before the office by petition as prescribed by the rules; and performs other duties necessary and required for the administration of the USPTO.

The work of examining applications for patents is divided among a number of examining technology centers (TCs), each TC having jurisdiction over certain assigned fields of technology. Each TC is headed by group directors and staffed by examiners and support staff. The examiners review applications for patents and determine whether patents can be granted. An appeal can be taken to the Board of Patent Appeals and Interferences for their decisions refusing to grant a patent, and a review by the director of the USPTO may be had on other matters by petition. The examiners also identify applications that claim the same invention and may initiate proceedings, known as interferences, to determine who was the first inventor.

Other offices perform various services, such as receiving and distributing mail, receiving new applications, handling sales of printed copies of patents, making copies of records, inspecting drawings, and recording assignments. At present, the USPTO has over 6,000 employees, of whom about half are examiners and others with technical and legal training. Patent applications are received at the rate of over 300,000 per year. The office receives over 5 million pieces of mail each year.

USPTO Upgrades

Being right at the center of technological change, the USPTO is itself becoming equipped to "manage in fast company" through a vast expansion of electronic services for applications management, including online services to applicants. They are moving into what is called the new "e-government" mode.

FAST-COMPANY MANAGEMENT

Distinctive Characteristics of Fast-Company High-Tech Management

What knowledge and skills do you need to hone as a technology manager, look for when recruiting one, or require as educational objectives in a managerial training program? Since we already have an abundance of books and courses on all of the traditional qualities of the effective manager—from expertise in the core tasks to motivation, leadership qualities, and so on (and frankly, a lot of them belabor the obvious)—we need not dwell on them here. Instead we offer commentary on the recurring qualities we have found in our experiences, our research, and the literature dealing with management involving science and technology.

The unique characteristics of high-tech management reflect especially the rapidly changing world of technology and its potential for commercialization. Amplifying these are the following 10 specific qualities (see also figure 5.1):

1. **Commercialization concept:** Essentially, what technology-based business am I in, and what are my definitions of success? How is my technology a source of wealth? What is my metric of wealth—not just dollars, but in what profits, enhanced corporate value, or cost efficiencies?

2. **Underlying science:** What is the key technology and scientific or theoretical context? Where is research emanating from? Does my company have its own R&D mandate?

3. **Primary and secondary markets:** Ranging from local, regional, and national to global, in which economies do we compete? How—if at all—does my company relate to globalization? These are important policy questions.

4. **Natural environmental impacts:** Does my company have likely physical environmental water, air, sounds, or visual impacts? How do the law or watchdog agencies see them?

Figure 5.1
Aspects of High-Tech Company Management.

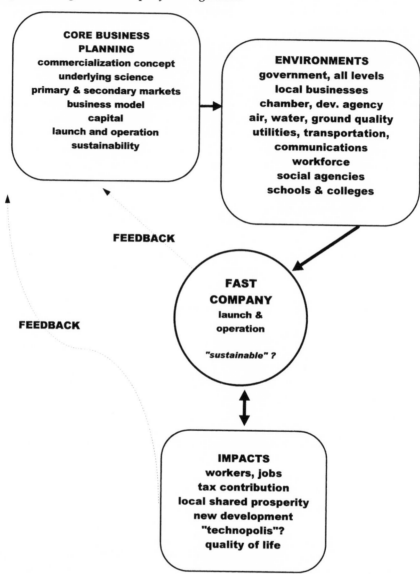

5. **Workforce impacts:** What are the qualities and special needs of my technology-oriented workforce? What kind of special workers do I need, where do I find them, and how do I train them? What assistance is available from local academic institutions? What occupational hazards are found in my line of work? Who is likely to monitor them?

6. **Socioeconomic impacts:** How might the presence or changes in operation affect the local socioeconomic environment—new job; better job; changes in

pay rates; benefits or work rules; or services from local agencies including schools, community colleges, and universities? Can I benefit from or contribute to new social or economic programs of the community?

7. **Governmental environment:** Considering benefits as well as barriers, beyond licensing and basic legal statutes, are there government programs (RFPs, economic development, training, environmental impact, business incubators, industrial parks) on the local, county, regional, state, federal, or international level that are particularly relevant to my business?

8. **Fast-company qualities:** What are the needed skills for rapid organizational change and adaptation, especially employing change or time as a competitive strategy? Can I beat my competition in time (e.g., the Zero Time concept)?

9. **Applied research tools:** The fast-company world of new technologies and varying commercial opportunities presents constant challenges for benchmarking, evaluating, weighing decisions, and estimating risk. Fortunately, many powerful research strategies are now available, and to compete, the technology manager must be able to not just understand their results but to call for and control their applications.

10. **Sustainability:** What qualities are critical for continuing my business? Can the basic model keep going or endure in our world of escalating change?

ZERO TIME

Fast-Company Management Priorities

As in the chapter title and above, please note that *Zero Time* is a proprietary concept; the trademark is held by Professor Raymond Yeh, who has commercialized the concept as a management strategy and offered documentation, consultancies, and training in the same. It is also the title of a book by Dr. Yeh with Keri Pearlson and George Kozmetsky.[1] Zero Time epitomizes how applications of technology, networking, and telecommunications can create the fast-company concept of the present book. Essentially, Yeh and his associates assert that the winning organizations of this age will gain their edge by accelerating reaction to change, often anticipating change before it happens. They have developed much of their approach from the study of such successful companies as Intel Corporation, Dell Computer Corporation, Amazon.com, and Ford Motor Company. These firms have been remarkably successful in closing "value gaps" between what the company thinks are the customers' values and what the customers actually want. Zero Time strategy requires identification of and concentration upon a firm's best customers, building long-term relations with them with a deep understanding and rapid alignment to these customers' values—the essence of the Zero Time concept.

Five Key Disciplines

Yeh and his colleagues describe five major actions, calling them *disciplines*, found in "near Zero Time" organizations. They include these concepts (their terms are in quotes; our descriptions are paraphrased[2]):

1. "Zero Value Gaps": Identify your key customers' values and gear your services or products specifically to address them.

2. "Zero Learning Gaps": Candidly develop and implement strategies for company learning processes—how to learn the values of customers and how to address them.

3. "Zero Management Gaps": Organize so that every subcomponent of company operations directly reflects the company's plan for action.

4. "Zero Process Gaps": Align operations so any barrier to Zero Time is removed or surmounted.

5. "Zero Inclusion Gaps": Insure that all central parties or components of your operation are included in key decision making.

Zero Time is a metaphorlike concept—one of tightening and accelerating the management process—like closing the gaps or white spaces in a flow chart or lags in a GANTT chart. An underlying premise, as I (FW) have written in prior books on technology-assisted management, is that acquisition of technology alone will not enhance performance. *Value is gained only from managing its extraction from the applications.*[3]

In concluding this chapter on the fast-company concept, we agree with Yeh and his associates that companies not able to work in Zero Time could well become extinct. Zero Time may be the best advice about inherently fast-company high-tech management of our time.

NOTES

1. Raymond Yeh, Keri Pearlson, and George Kozmetsky, *Zero Time: Providing Instant Customer Value—Every Time, All the Time* (New York: Wiley, 2000).

2. Yeh, Pearlson, and Kozmetsky, *Zero Time*. These constitute the organizing scheme of their book, giving for each the concept, company examples, and advice for implementation—all very action-oriented and, unlike some business books, specific, informative, and not altogether obvious.

3. For example, see Frederick Williams and Herbert S. Dordick, *The Executive's Guide to Information Technology* (New York: Wiley, 1983); Herbert S. Dordick and Frederick Williams, *Innovative Management Using Telecommunications* (New York: Wiley, 1986).

CHAPTER 6

Progress in Networks and Networking

Business and economic development research over the past three decades has repeatedly demonstrated the importance of networks and networking. From their core structures to operation in the worlds of commerce, all businesses are essentially multilayered networks—centripetally in their core operations and centrifugally as they depend upon linkages with their markets, suppliers, and the myriad of financial and transportation services. In this chapter we examine concepts and selected advances of network theory relative to their uses in studying the commercialization of marketing of science and technology. This forms a basis for the introduction in chapter 6 of the idealized local developmental network, or *technopolis*, as we have called it.

ENTREPRENEURIAL NETWORKS

Research into the sociology of the entrepreneurial process has revealed that within complex networks of relationships, entrepreneurship is facilitated or constrained by linkages between aspiring entrepreneurs, resources, and opportunities, and reflects the interaction of chance, necessity, and purpose in all social action. Hence, comprehensive explanations of entrepreneurship must include the social context of behavior, especially the social relationships through which people obtain information, resources, and social support. There is also an important set of connections among elements of the innovation process that involve contacts, collaborations, and movements among people. The power of these connections has been stressed in numerous reports on research collaborations.

People are themselves repositories of knowledge. They can also guide others to information resources in their fields that otherwise would remain unknown, buried, or forbidden. Furthermore, people know more than they can say, and possess skills as well as knowledge. The only way to communicate such tacit knowledge and know-how from one institution or one part of the innovation process to another is for people to learn from each other and move from one locus to another. Institutional ties and arrangements facilitate such people-to-people connections. The more such people-to-people and institutional connections we can establish, the stronger and the more extensive we can make them; and the more commercial-sector, institutional, R&D-spectrum, and disciplinary lines they cross, the stronger will be our scientific and technical enterprise.

The most important conditions for homegrown high-technology development are the entrepreneurial network and the supporting computer/telecommunications infrastructure that facilitate the creation of indigenous high-technology firms and support their survival.

NOTES ON NETWORK THEORY

Underlying Processes and Principles

As Peter Monge and Noshir Contractor, in their recent *Theories of Network Communication,*[1] so realistically explain, we have too long looked at networks superficially at the expense of searching for underlying principles, evidence for which is so prevalent. In our presently limited space, we will attempt a few notes on the concepts of network theory and their advances, especially as could benefit technology-based entrepreneurship. Figure 6.1 lays out a few introductory concepts necessary for our discussion of the processes and principles of network operation.

The Graph

Basically, a network (or *graph,* as is sometimes used) is a collection of entities that can potentially link (i.e., interact, communicate, affect, interrelate) with one another. These entities—called *nodes*—could be folks at a cocktail party, neurons in our central nervous system, or the neurons of a simple worm. Nodes can be places or users of the Internet, or the ants killing my lawn. So, essentially, we are talking about collections of nodes and links.

Links, Density, and Degrees of Separation

As illustrated in figure 6.1, a node might not link to anything or anyone; as such, it's an *isolate*. But it is more likely for nodes to be interlinked, as with the dyad, triad, quad, and so on that are shown. Obviously, the more nodes, the more potential links. One can easily envisage how a network

Figure 6.1
Graphs of Links and Nodes.

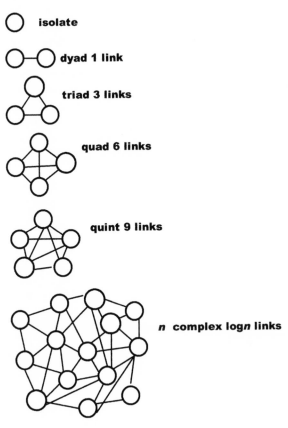

or graph may vary in density, a function of the number of nodes and the proportion that are actually linked. In fact, the ratio of the number of linked nodes divided by the number of nodes yields a coefficient of clustering where 0 is none and 1.0 is the maximum. Lest this begin to sound overly abstract, imagine the first meeting of a university class of, say, 80 students. If this were a class drawing students from different majors and from across a large campus, it might be that no more than four or five had ever talked to one another (a possible simple definition of link, for now); if five, the coefficient (rounded) would be .06—pretty low. Skip to the last class meeting, where after 15 weeks the situation is about reverse—say, 75 of the 80 have talked at least once—and the clustering coefficient has leaped to .94. In discussing links students made over the semester, you would probably find numerous cases where Sam may not be able to say that he talked with Sarah, but could maintain that he "knows her" through Mary, whom he talks with now and then. Sure, he can get a message to Sarah: he'll give it to Mary. A lot of linkages are not direct; they have an intermediary or intermediaries, which in network theory are called *degrees of separation*. Sam knows Mary directly, so there are no (or zero) degrees of separation, but Mary is between him and Sara, or one degree of separation. Sam might also say that he can claim a linkage through Mary to Sarah to the university president, Dr. Yale, whose daughter, Phyllis, in turn is Sarah's friend; thus he is three degrees of separation (Mary-Sarah-Phyllis) from his school's chief officer. Literature reviewed by Monge and Contractor as well as by Barabasi[2] provides numerous examples of degrees of separation, including firm reason to believe that most of us on this earth are divided by up to six degrees of separation.[3]

Small Worlds

Perhaps you can recall at some time saying, "It's a small world," or something similar, when discovering that you and another person have a friend or business contact in common. This phenomenon reflects two characteristics of common networks. First, most of us belong to a variety of small groups or complete networks (or graphs) of mostly strong ties, as with close family, associates at work, or colleagues in a professional field for sports teams. There are indeed small worlds, but they are not usually limited in and of themselves. Indeed, individuals (or nodes) often have links with individuals in other groups; they can be strong links, but more often these intergroup links can be weak ones. They do not require the presence, attention, or expense of constant or intense activity. We use them only when we need and can find them. For example, it is easy for one to locate and double-check a GDP-per-capita figure in the *CIA Factbook*, a database from the *Economist*, or some United Nations' report, mostly all direct links. But in the past, I (FW) have sought additional information and needed something other than my usual source. In one case it was to double-check on the GDP per capita for Cuba ($1,700 in the *Factbook*), the country's population (12 million), and GDP ($19.2 billion). So I telephoned a Cuban economist I had met at a conference in Havana, a contact one could liken to an "occasional link" since I do not regularly communicate or deal with him. He explained that for security reasons they do not release their figures, least of all to the American Central Intelligence Agency! He, like myself, works within a tightly linked network, or cluster, of colleagues—our respective small worlds. However, our person-to-person contact also links our two worlds, an example of how an occasional or weak link creates another small-world phenomenon involving quite different networks or clusters. Figure 6.2 illustrates this phenomenon for multiple small-world clusters; note the arcs designating occasional or weak links. Much of society, organizations, or entire systems of commerce

Figure 6.2
Small Worlds. Clusters with strong ties and clusters with weak ties.

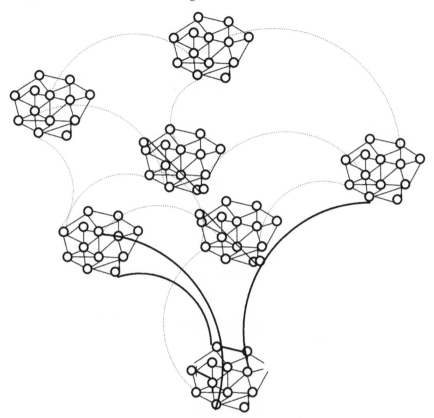

have this quality, and so does the type of network environments we research or design for economic development.

Summary Notes

1. In economic studies we find that virtually all development involves the evolution of a multilevel network phenomena—the interaction of agents evolving into a network or complementarities of mutual assistance.

2. For successful economic development, the fundamental developmental network is often one of cooperation: partnership among government, business, academia, and facilitating organizations (e.g., chambers of commerce) as cooperating entities.

3. Within most of these base components (government, etc.), there is a primary, supporting centripetal network.

4. As developmental cooperation proceeds, the primary, base-component centripetal networks link centrifugally, eventually forming larger, grand networks.

5. Principles of network theory apply and are a basis for description, research, explanation, and eventually policy and planning for business and economic development.

6. Practically speaking, most economic development is, structurally, a network phenomenon.

7. Therefore, network theory, as described by scientists such as Peter Monge and Noshir Contractor in *Theories of Communication Networks*[4] and Albert-Laszlo Barabasi in *Linked: The New Science of Networks*[5] can benefit substantially the analysis and planning of business and economic development.

NOTES

1. Peter R. Monge and Noshir S. Contractor, *Theories of Network Communication* (Oxford: Oxford University Press, 2004).

2. Albert-Laszlo Barabasi, *Linked: The New Science of Networks* (Cambridge, Mass.: Perseus Publishing, 2002).

3. In my (FW) mother's family (Elder) there was handed down a list of mostly second and third cousins (maybe five degrees of separation) through whom we could claim a distant relation to General Robert E. Lee, leader of the Southern armies in the American Civil War. Added to this was a further possible link to George Washington, a daughter of whom they thought had became Lee's wife. But research by one of our family revealed that George and Martha Washington had no children together. She married him as a young widow with two children, one a daughter (Martha "Patsy" Parke Custis), whose daughter's daughter (George's great-step-grandchild, Mary Anna Rudolf) in turn married Robert E. Lee. How about saying that I am related by n degrees of separation to George Washington?

4. Monge and Contractor, *Theories of Network Communication*.

5. Barabasi, *Linked*.

CHAPTER 7

Learning amid, for, and Using Technology

We have chosen to call this a *learning* rather than an *education* chapter because, to us, learning focuses on the bottom line—namely, the acquisition of knowledge, skills, strategies, and values. You cannot survive in our era of perpetual technological change without a substantial commitment to learning—especially on the part of investors, entrepreneurs, managers, supervisors, and workers. And this includes the learning challenges to companies themselves. As we reintroduced in chapter 5 and discuss further here, in order to compete, fast companies must be learning companies.

Also, there is the admonition to use technology for learning in the age of science and technology. We address this point in this chapter with selected commentary on the concept and practice of distance education.

LEGACY OF PUBLIC EDUCATION AND THE NEW CHALLENGES

Historical Perspective

Among the great American success stories is that of public education. Author of the Declaration of Independence and our third president, Thomas Jefferson (1743–1826) envisioned the U.S. public education system as the fountainhead of democracy. The purpose of public schools was to create civil and capable citizens. For democracy to succeed, the participation of an educated and efficacious public is required. by the people, for the people. Jefferson, a lifelong advocate of learning and discovery, commissioned in 1803 America's Corps of Discovery, best known to most today as the expedition led by Captains Meriwether Lewis and William Clark to explore the country west of the Mississippi, to map, document, and find an overland route to the Pacific Ocean. Truly, this was a nineteenth-century version of R&D.

New Challenges: Transformation of Knowledge into Value

In our newest century, education and training are especially differentiated in the presumptions that although education can provide knowledge, an individual must convert that knowledge into value, whereas training itself is knowledge with immediate market value. As public education has aimed to provide basic knowledge and skills to all people, it remains for the individual to use this foundation to actualize personal ambitions in the open market of opportunity.

Need to Keep Pace with Economic Change

Although founded during an agricultural age, the U.S. public education system continued to function and serve during the industrial era. But now, in a new era of burgeoning growth in science and technology where these is a stress upon knowledge creation and technology innovation, public education is being challenged to respond effectively to the accelerated pace of economic and societal change. Rather than broad criticism, complaints about "failing schools," or other inadequacies in opportunities for learning, any society anxious to take advantage of developmental opportunities of science and technology must sharpen its focus on education and instructional updates to serve in the new era. Not only do we need curriculum reviews to update and upgrade existing instructional levels and topics so as to better serve one's society and economy, but we must also ask whether we can or should offer more learning opportunities directly in the concepts and practices of enterprise and entrepreneurship.

USE TECHNOLOGY TO TEACH TECHNOLOGY

Start Young

Why not explore more uses of science and technology to amplify these new learning opportunities? Following are topics and projects we have found valuable for training the twenty-first-century workforce—for example, adding enterprise and entrepreneurship to the K–12 curriculum. As educational planners will tell you, many curriculum topics can begin with the youngest of schoolchildren, often the younger the better. Here are suggestions about commerce and enterprise that we have culled from experience and the literature.

Learning Objectives in K through Primary Grades

Your coauthor (FW) remembers that on his first day in kindergarten, the teacher had the 20 or so boys and girls use large wooden play blocks to lay out the shape of a popcorn stand. We teamed up to make a large batch of popcorn, divided it into small bags, then opened the stand "for business." We took turns buying the bags until we invited the class in from the room next door. They ate us out of business. I think we learned not only about supply and demand that day; consider how the following could be integrated into the social-studies curriculum:

- What is *doing business?*
- How do people fit into businesses—that is, as worker, boss, owner, developer, or entrepreneur?
- Where do you want to fit and why?
- Why is business important to you and your community?

Middle and High School

When subjects begin to be important to a young person's consideration of role models, experiences, lifestyles, or career choices, middle school can provide excellent opportunities for introducing relevant subjects. Research indicates that sex-role stereotyping of careers may inhibit young females' motivations to study mathematics and science.[1] Some middle and high school topics—note their personal angle—include the following:

- **Commerce:** What is commerce, and how has it been a key factor in history?
- **Value sources:** What are the various sources of value extracted from nature, as with petroleum, mining, hunting, fishing, or water? How does value come from manufacturing? Is there a knowledge economy? Would you like a job in it? Which job?
- **Political economies:** Distinguish among capitalism, socialism, and communism.
- **Profit:** What is it? Who deserves it?
- **Entrepreneurship:** What does an entrepreneur do, and what are key qualities of entrepreneurship or of an entrepreneur?
- **Business:** How do you start a business?
- **Careers:** What are they, and what would you like yours to be?
- **Career preparation:** How can you prepare for your career choice?
- **Multiple careers:** It is likely you will have multiple careers; what might they be?
- **Multiskilling:** What is it, and why is it important today?

- **Sex-role stereotypes:** What are some, and why should you avoid them? Avoid sex-role stereotyping about careers.[2]

High School and Beyond

In all, we seek to develop those skills, competencies, understandings, and attributes that prepare young workers, aspiring managers, or entrepreneurs to be innovative; we want young people to develop the critical skills needed for teamwork, commitment, and flexibility. Students will benefit from a realistic knowledge and understanding of business and work opportunities, including starting their own business. Therefore, why not design a specialty in high school for entrepreneurship, like we have in technology and the performing arts? Use technology to teach technology and innovation. Try for a model program demonstrating a transferable model with cost-benefits from employing

- multimedia,
- Internet online pages,
- weekly pep meeting in rented movie theaters,
- and as much university and business cooperation as possible.

Online Internet-based curricula were contributed by outside agencies and organizations, such as the Kids' Pages described in chapter 5 from the United States Patent and Trademark Office. These pages can serve as a *learning module*, directly applicable to a civics course in a grade or high school.

Direct Preparation for the Tech Workforce: The EnterTech Project

Need

Central Texas had the dilemma in the 1980s where the growth of high-tech industry was beginning to outstrip the supply of shop-floor workers. The University of Texas IC[2] Institute, working with the Governor's Science and Technology Council, surveyed selected technology companies, asking what they looked for in recruiting young workers. The results led to the development of a computer-assisted curriculum specifically oriented to enter technology jobs—thus its name, *EnterTech.* As of this writing, its formal description is

The 45-hour EnterTech program is an instructor-led Web based workforce training program that simulates "on-the-job" experiences and rapidly imparts crucial personal growth and development skills. Since the EnterTech program successfully teaches employability skills, graduates experience higher incomes, job promotions, improved confidence and a desire to continue their education.

EnterTech Learning Goals

Below, for illustration, we have paraphrased major EnterTech learning goals, but not the entire formal list, which could change:

1. **Do the job:** Basically, be able to perform the work, understand and follow job handbooks, and understand quality safety requirements.
2. **Appropriate dress and behavior.**
3. **Organizational skills:** Develop abilities in identifying, remembering, and processing information.
4. **Speaking:** Increase skills in being able to speak clearly and concisely to convey information and answer questions.
5. **Reading:** Acquire skills relevant to understanding written work orders and interpreting graphs.
6. **Writing:** Be able to record and organize written information, have basic numerical and arithmetic skills, and understand simple calculations such as counting and weighing product and calculating postage.
7. **Problem solving:** Employ basic strategies such as defining the problem, sensing alternative solutions, and evaluating solutions that were applied.
8. **Learn on the job:** Gain skills and assist others with learning—in all, "growth" skills.

What's Next for EnterTech?

There have been and will continue to be more field applications. A school district or any sponsoring entity can license use of the program. Recently, more of the materials have been made available for Web site presentation. Now noteworthy, we believe, are ongoing translations of the materials in Spanish and Portuguese for trial uses in Mexico and Brazil. We know that EnterTech works and can be transferred to many environments. Therefore, any group wishing to promote their own worker-readiness skills for technological employment should examine EnterTech or perhaps create their own, if cost-effective. "EnterTech is real and it works" is so often said by users.

Manufacturing Technology Laboratory (MTL)

Concept

Essentially, the MTL is a large trailer equipped to demonstrate hands-on design and related manufacturing processes; it can be towed to participating schools who may not be able to afford such facilities.

Origin

In 1995, an education committee of the National Center for Manufacturing Sciences (NCMS) in Ann Arbor, Michigan, took the position that students, beginning in grade school, could benefit from a more hands-on approach to learning how the traditional three Rs of reading, writing, and arithmetic were important in everyday life, especially for holding a job someday in manufacturing. They also saw the need for students to experience concretely how computers could be used to design and build products. Unfortunately, public schools often lacked the ability to offer such learning experiences. Their brainchild was to design a mobile laboratory—eventually an enclosed trailer that could be pulled by a heavy-duty pickup truck—within which students could design simple objects (keychain holders, chess pieces, name plates, etc.) that then could be produced on the spot in a plastic molding machine. Thus the students could see the manufacturing process from design to product, and even take the product home with them. NCMS describes how the MTL brings state-of-the-art technology directly to schools in the form of a mobile unit equipped to provide hands-on experience in computer-aided manufacturing technologies. The primary goal of the MTL program is to provide learning opportunities for students to acquire the cognitive skills required to achieve technological literacy. A complementary goal is to prepare K-14 teachers by providing teacher training in the MTL program. Teachers present various topics in the classroom and students work on MTL provided computers to design their projects. The MTL mobile unit soon arrives on campus for a two-week stay, and students take their designs, stored on floppy, to the lab where they use computer controlled lathe milling machines and robot to actually manufacture what they have designed in class.

GRADUATE MS PROGRAM IN SCIENCE AND TECHNOLOGY COMMERCIALIZATION

Beginnings

A major dividend of the industrial boom in microelectronics commercialization during the 1980s was to design university curricula with learning objectives in the nature and practice of the commercialization of science and technology. The strategy of the IC^2 Institute, with over 25 years experience of research and projects in this area, was to design a 12-month master's degree program, which became known as the Master of Science in Science and Technology Commercialization (MSSTC).

The degree was formally approved as an MS program authorized by the University of Texas Graduate Curriculum Committee. The decision to offer a degree package was motivated by several concerns, namely that students ought to have an option to pursue these skills for both graduate credit and an MS degree rather than a certificated program of some type. A formal degree is a solid résumé entry, can add to deciding an individual's rank and salary in a firm, and positions tuition costs (originally about $18,000) favorably for tax or reimbursement purposes, the latter sometimes by a student's employer. The program had to be entirely self-supporting. It was initially offered on the Austin campus and simultaneously in Arlington, Virginia. It was also decided early on to develop multimedia learning materials, including videotape, video teleconferencing, and (as it became available a year or so later) the Internet. Today, the entire program can be taken online.

Description

In printed material and a dedicated Web site, the program is described as follows:

The MSSTC is a 12-month program designed for working professionals who want to become change catalysts for the improvement of technology commercialization processes. Successful graduates are equipped to make informed technology management and planning decisions. If you want to learn how to start and operate high technology ventures, either as new start-ups or spin-offs, or within an existing organization, this is the program for you.

Curriculum

This section presents a summary of the 12 courses constituting the University of Texas IC^2 Institute MSSTC degree program. Each course is 3 credit hours.

STC 380: Converting Technology to Wealth. Examine how technology is converted to wealth through the commercialization process.

Areas of Focus

- Issues involved in the entire technology commercialization process
- The importance of technology commercialization to economic development
- How to assess a technology for its commercial value

STC 382: Marketing Technological Innovations. Develop an understanding of the forces driving competition and demand in markets or technology-intensive products and services.

Areas of Focus

- The importance of a customer focus as opposed to a technology focus
- How to apply marketing principles to the commercialization process

- Skills in launching, promoting, pricing, and distributing high-technology products

STC 383: Technology Management and Transfer: Theory and Practice. Address the evaluation, formulation, and use of technology transfer models.

Areas of Focus

- How to formulate, evaluate, and use models of stakeholders, success factors, and barriers to accelerate knowledge and technology transfer and application
- How to document and critically evaluate key knowledge/technology management processes in specific national and global contexts
- How government policies affect commercialization of R&D, especially in universities, national laboratories, consortia, and small companies

STC 386T1: Financing New Ventures. Learn financial planning, methods for determining capital requirements, and various ways of financing growth and making investment decisions.

Areas of Focus

- The key differences between large and small businesses and procedures for starting a new venture
- How to manage financial resources, make financial projections, and value a new venture
- The importance of linking strategy to finance in a new venture

STC 384: Commercialization Strategy. Gain an understanding of technology and commercialization strategies as a part of business strategy.

Areas of Focus

- The various levels of strategy and how to position commercialization and technology strategy within the business strategy of an enterprise
- How to perform an analysis of an industry and how to identify and maximize the use of core competencies
- How to develop a commercialization strategy and how to position products and services relative to competition in an industry

STC 386T2: Risk Analysis. Explore decision and risk analysis, methods for structuring and modeling decision problems, and an application of methods to a variety of problems.

Areas of Focus

- The basic tools available for structuring problems involving risk and uncertainty

- How to apply these tools to the analysis of problems involving risk and uncertainty

STC 394c: Managing Product Development and Production. Examine the many and best practices organizations are using to accelerate the product-development and production processes.

Areas of Focus

- The processes of product development and production, including how to accelerate and otherwise improve these processes
- Enhanced skills in project management and process-flow analysis and design
- Key issues involved in lean production, mass customization, and supply-chain management

STC 395: The Art and Science of Market-Driven Entrepreneurship. Learn the process of creating new ventures, the dynamics of growth-oriented firms, and the roles of entrepreneurs and investors.

Areas of Focus

- How to identify and determine what managers need to know about the critical driving forces in a new venture success
- How successful entrepreneurs and investors create and build value for themselves and others
- The financial and nonfinancial resources necessary for new ventures and how to identify the criteria used to screen and evaluate proposals

STC 381: Legal Issues of the Commercialization Process. Examine the numerous legal challenges organizations face as they commercialize technology in a global environment.

Areas of Focus

- The general processes of converting knowledge and technology to rationally valued intellectual property via copyrights, patents, and trademarks
- The ownership and financial resource implications for various legal forms of organizations
- Issues involved in shareholder buy and sell agreements, management team agreements, employee stock options, licensing, and joint development agreements

STC 385: Creative and Innovative Management. Learn to apply new concepts and ideas, initiatives, and methods that can be used to provide new directions or modes of operation for organizations and activities.

Areas of Focus

- Factors and leadership behaviors that enable creativity and innovation in organizations
- The nature of team leadership and team dynamics in assuring creative collaboration
- Methods to successfully lead change and persuasively advocate ideas
- Handling organizational crises and difficult management problems and building both employee and customer loyalty

STC 391: Internationalization of Technology. Explore a broad set of issues of commercializing technology on a global scale.

Areas of Focus

- Information resources essential to the practice of international commercialization of technology
- How macro historical and current forces affect global commercialization processes
- Practical microprocesses of commercializing technologies, including partnering, business and tax structures, financing, marketing, cultural acclimatization, country policies, and trade issues

STC 396: Technology Enterprise Design and Implementation. Develop a multidisciplinary approach to the preparation and presentation of a detailed, growth-oriented business plan for a technology enterprise or project.

Areas of Focus

- How to create and present a business plan for a new venture
- How to determine the critical tasks to be accomplished during start-up and early growth and what is necessary for success
- How to identify decisions that can increase the reward-to-risk ratio at various stages of the company's growth

Distance Education

Delivering educational material to the student, whether by mail, radio, television, or the Internet, is what distance education is all about. The practice dates back to the 1880s, when the Australians had a system of delivering printed school lessons to persons living in the outback. Since the turn of the century, most industrialized nations have had one type or another of correspondence courses. Broadcasting became a high-visibility component of distance education with the development of Britain's Open University in the 1960s, where educational programming was combined with mail-based correspondence courses.

In the United States we have seen many and varied applications of distance education. For example, telephone companies have long made available "home instruction" links whereby bedridden children could interact with their classrooms. On a much larger scale have been the development of radio-based networks as in the states of Wisconsin or Texas, a "University of the Air" that operated out of Nebraska, and Instructional Television Fixed Service (ITFS) where lectures are broadcast in a limited-range area and students may interact via a telephone-based audio link. The latter has been used quite successfully in the dissemination of engineering courses to students on-site at companies, as in programs operated by Stanford University and the University of Southern California. Although there have been several major initiatives to develop an institution in the United States similar to Britain's Open University, a comparable major system has never been accomplished. There are many opinions on this matter, but a common one is that with our extensive system of community colleges and state universities, students have more of an opportunity to go to a nearby campus than do students in Great Britain.

The aforementioned ITFS services for engineers and scientists on the job are the closest major example for earlier programs in science and technology education. Today there are many individual services offered by universities or commercial institutions. Some have advanced to video teleconferencing, but in the last decade, the Internet has become a popular medium for distance education. Because the situation is so fast-changing, rather than try to enumerate many examples in the present space, your best opportunities to find courses would be to contact local colleges and universities, as well, of course, as to search the Internet for announcements or the courses themselves.

NOTES

1. Cf. Frederick Williams, Robert LaRose, and Fredericka Frost, *Children, Television, and Sex-Role Stereotyping* (New York: Praeger, 1981).

2. EnterTech has been well documented; information can be accessed via the IC² Institute Web site (http://www.ic2.org/) or by contacting the organization. We wish to give credit to those who led and developed the project, including Deaton Bender, Melinda Jackson, and Aimee Boyd, who conducted an extensive and summative field evaluation.

CHAPTER 8

Creating the Technopolis

A major research program at IC^2 has been studying enterprise creation in local regions. This is commensurate with our premise of "think globally, act locally." In today's economy, everything is in a global context, yet action is best started at home, where one has control over resources and direction. To initiate enterprise, we need to recruit and leverage the components of smart infrastructure—that is, talent, technology, innovation, capital, and know-how. We typically find these components in local institutions of business, government, and universities. The process of local development begins with cooperation among them—a kind of strong-tie, small-world network, or graph, as introduced in chapter 6. Eventually, this cooperative network may grow to a mature enterprising and living environment we call the *technopolis*, a topic pursued further in this chapter. A technopolis, or technopoleis (plural), may also reach out through occasional links or weak ties.

SMART INFRASTRUCTURE

Lest it is not becoming obvious in this discussion, a winning strategy for local development of a given technology-based business or commercial sector begins with local networking of resources and leadership, which, again, we often refer to as *smart infrastructure*—or the foundation for building the technopolis. This group may, in turn, seek cooperation with other such groups.

For the time being, let us review five key factors: (1) talent, (2) technology, (3) innovation, (4) capital, and (5) know-how.

THE FIVE KEY FACTORS FOR DEVELOPMENT

1. Talent

The pool of entrepreneurial talent is dependent on a number of variables. The entrepreneurial climate of a region may be a particularly critical variable influencing entrepreneurship—namely, well-connected networks of individuals and organizations, previous entrepreneurs, encouragement for innovative activity, and risk taking. Environmental conditions that foster high rates of technology entrepreneurship tend to be local attributes: improvements in local infrastructure (utilities, roads, schools, and other public facilities), access to other areas, and quality of life within a region, and the interrelatedness of (1) the functions of firms and their innovative activities, (2) the firm-to-firm flow of information, and (3) how the entrepreneurial history and climate interact to bring about and bolster economic growth and development.

Entrepreneurs face personal pushes and pulls that affect their decision to start a company. Pushes can result from the outright loss of a job, or from discontent at work because an idea is rejected, a career is stymied, or the future is perceived as insecure or unpromising. Pulls include a desire for independence, a chance to pursue an idea, an opportunity for greater financial rewards, a perception of excitement, or an apparent market opportunity. These pull factors are influenced by various personal characteristics. Some characteristics that recur in research on entrepreneurs include the need for advancement, a desire to control and direct, a propensity for taking calculated risks, and a problem-solving style. Despite the list of characteristics, entrepreneurs tend to be quite diverse, and no one set of characteristics describes them all. There is another and more important characteristic, however, that does seem to have a powerful influence on one's decision to start a company—namely, the presence of role models or mentors who, through their own entrepreneurial activities, present an effective example for would-be entrepreneurs.

2. Technology

The development of technology, the second essential factor, is dependent on situational conditions. Technology is generated by a variety of R&D performers—universities, large technology companies, government and private-sector research laboratories, technical institutes, small companies, and inventors. Each of these performers may have quite different organizational cultures and missions, policies and procedures, and goals and expectations. The contemporary environment yields an explosive growth of scientific and technical knowledge. This is coupled with an increase in professionals with expertise in these areas and an expanding means to transfer and share this knowledge. The very nature of technological innovation poses a unique set of conditions for the commercialization of technology.

3. Innovation

Technical innovations often result in a gap between the technology on one hand and the market on the other. The gap arises because of two different perspectives. On the side of those who produce the technology, there is a great understanding of the technology. This intrinsic understanding leads to high interest in the innovation and a desire to push something new into the marketplace. Potential users or buyers, on the other hand, often lack intrinsic knowledge about the technology, may be uninformed, or may have various levels of sophistication in understanding. Consequently, they have lower interest in trying something new. They tend to be satisfied with what they have been previously using and extremely concerned about cost.

Bridging this gap requires a new way of thinking about the commercialization of technological innovations. The more technologically innovative the product or service, the less effective traditional approaches to the market tend to be. For example, forecasting demand for technological innovations is difficult because potential buyers may not have a clear frame of reference for the new technology and its utilization. In addition, for many innovations, applications may be uncertain and cut across a variety of industries. For traditional products and services, product life cycles may be 20, 30, or 40 years once they are introduced into the market. With technological innovations, a product may have no more than 18 months before technical obsolescence, competition, or changing needs alter the market, so speed of development poses special problems in going to market. Finally, there is reluctance to buy early-generation technologies. Potential buyers tend to wait for later generations, with the feeling that the technology will work better and cost less.

4. Capital

Capital may be the most elusive factor in the promotion of technological activities. The elusiveness stems from the diverse nature of the commodity and its sources of supply. Yet capital is a critical infrastructure element for new technology and new company development. Capital formation consists of those private-capital institutions that have been established to generate profits and those technology-venturing institutions that reflect new types of collaboration among business, government, and academia to promote economic development.

In considering patterns of investment, there is a correlation between stages of growth and appropriate sources of capital. In the seed or start-up stage, the entrepreneur tends to use his own funds and those of family and friends. Because for most entrepreneurs these funds are quite limited, the search for capital then becomes more challenging, complex, and uncertain. Private, affluent investors or business angels can be an important source of seed capital. But linking the entrepreneur with these investors has been a difficult problem, since this investor marketplace has been misunderstood, invisible to most entrepreneurs, and thus highly inefficient. If the company has the potential for growth, then future financing sources may be banks and other commercial lenders, small-business investment companies, venture-capital firms, and various types of government funding. More dynamic companies may tap other sources of funding in additional rounds of financing designed to help accelerate growth. These include public equity offerings, venture-capital companies, and large financial institutions. Each of these capital sources has its own sets of investment criteria, objectives, and requirements. And each imposes important sets of requirements on entrepreneurs and their companies.

5. Know-How

The final factor, know-how, may be the most critical in influencing the promotion and commercialization of technological activities. Expertise and experience involving management, marketing, finance, production, and manufacturing as well as legal, scientific, and engineering expertise is at the center of a core of studies relating to new-venture success/failure in high-technology start-ups and to the commercialization of technology. Factors such as prior experience in markets or technologies, the founder's education level, team development, previous managerial experience in high-growth and well-managed companies, and marketing prowess all attest to the importance of business and technical know-how. The viability of a smart infrastructure tends to be highly dependent on a region's business and technical know-how or its access to them.

THE TECHNOPOLIS NETWORK

As we said earlier, recruitment of, and cooperation among, the key components for development are achieved by strong local networking, coupled with advice or assistance obtained from resources outside the locale—the typical weak-tie linkage.

Figure 8.1 shows a basic local technopolis network and also notes how this network, graph, or group may network beyond their usual boundaries. Important characteristics of this figure are as follows:

- Key players—businesses, universities, government, and entrepreneurs—united in concern for new technology are a care network; their linkages are interactive.
- The straight lines and arrows represent strong ties. That is, these nodes are often and reliably in communication with one another. Communication is easy, in-

Figure 8.1
Technopolis Network. © **1999 The IC²** Institute. © 2003 revision George Kozmetsky and Frederick Williams.

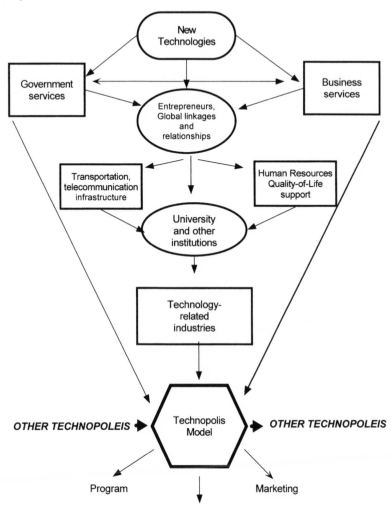

expensive, and offers the preferred medium—as with telephone, fax, e-mail, videoconferencing, postal mail, or even face-to-face meetings. Security may be an important requirement. In all, the basic players must be in as close touch as they wish with one another. Weak ties, or occasional communication, as shown by the arcs (dashes), are also an important component; in this case we show them connecting technopolis-management units.

- The valued technologies may be recently invented, enhanced, or obtained from outside sources (*technology transfer*, chapter 10).

- The commercialization process is undertaken by technology-related industries, themselves dependent upon human resources and quality of life as well as transportation and communication systems.

- Technopolis management not only oversees the local network but can itself serve as a node on a larger graph—that is, with other technopoleis. As with the example in chapter 17, about Project Caribe, technopolis construction in the region should look to links with major foreign resource centers as well as among themselves. Technopoleis of the Caribbean could be a single, grand technopolis as linkages are firmed. In such a case, part of the transformation would be to transform the management-unit weak ties into strong ones.

- Directors, ministers, or officers planning and managing economic development use the technopolis network as a planning aid.

- Aspiring entrepreneurs can plot their most advantageous uses of the local technopolis network.

- The network concept offers scalability—as in applications, locally, regionally, or internationally.

- Evolving network theory offers a wealth of ideas for designing, improving, and managing technopolis-oriented developmental projects.

CHAPTER 9

Adoption of Innovations

The process of the flow and adoption of innovations has a theoretical history in the works of Everett Rogers, well summed up in his diffusion of innovations. Knowledge about change and the ways of achieving it are very much a communication process. The theory applies not only to individuals, but to groups and organizations, businesses, and even governments. Rogers' diffusion is the process by which an innovation is communicated through certain channels over time among the members of a social system.

The pattern of adoption can be illustrated by an S curve, such as the one illustrated in figure 9.1. The vertical axis is the percentage of adopters; the horizontal is time.

As shown in the curve, adoption starts with no or very few adopters (left, bottom of curve). As the innovation begins to have more adopters, the curve swings up and continues across time until it levels out with the maximum percentage of adopters. This S curve has been found in many studies, including the adoption of farming methods, family planning methods, and even color TV sets. In any changing society, including the Caribbean, we would expect to see this pattern in adoption of innovations.

The vertical axis is the percentage of adopters (1 = 100%). The horizontal axis is time (months, quarters, or whatever). This illustrates an often-found relationship (the S curve) of the adoption of an innovation across time.

Some entities are *early adopters*, who are characteristically on the lookout for new concepts, methods, and know-how. It is the kind of knowledge

Figure 9.1
The S Diffusion Curve. Also called an *adoption curve*. The vertical axis is percentage of adopters (1 = 100%); the horizontal axis is time (months, quarters, or whatever). This illustrates an often-found relationship (S curve) of the adoption of an innovation across time.

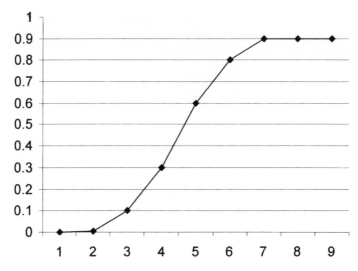

described earlier. Early adopters are flexible and progressive in their actions. At the opposite end are *laggards*, the individuals or entities who are slow to change, or do not change at all. They are frequently out of the communications loop either by design or by the lack of the capability to join it. Laggards also typically resist change out of clinging to tradition, being naysayers, fearing the new, or holding rational beliefs in the disadvantages in change. In today's telecommunications, the concept of an intelligent network offers the smart infrastructure that obviates knowledge networks and capabilities for change. They support the assets of knowledge and information as introduced in chapter 1. In a broad sense, technopoleis and their networks are platforms for the diffusion of innovations.

BENCHMARKING CHANGE

Considering the high costs involved and the importance of success in promoting the adoption of innovations, it is imperative to have a means to measure change. Where are you now? Where do you want to go? How will you know when you get there?

These are known as *benchmark studies*. The best and most objective studies look for hard data, not just opinions or other qualitative observations. Data can be both investment input and performance output as seen across

Figure 9.2
Hypothetical Time-Series Analysis of Effects of Jobs Created. The vertical axis is both investment amount (1 = $100,000) and number of jobs created (1 = 100); The horizontal axis is time (in months). The bottom curve shows investment amount; the top curve shows change in jobs created. In this case, the analysis illustrates small or no effect in jobs created.

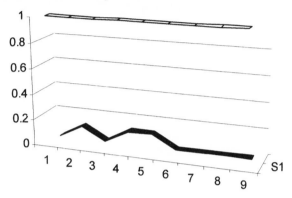

Figure 9.3
Hypothetical Time-Series Analysis of Effects of Jobs Created from Investment in Business Incubator. The bottom curve shows investment amount (1 = $100,000); the top curve shows change in jobs created (1 = 100). This illustrates the effect of a boost in incubator investment (bottom curve) upon growth in jobs created (top curve). It also illustrates the "lagged" effect across time of job increase coming after incubator investment.

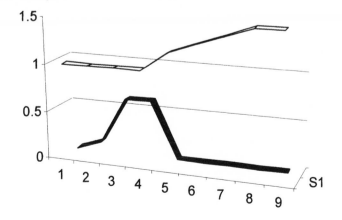

time. For example, has investment in a business incubator (input) resulted in new jobs? Examine figures 9.2 and 9.3. Both are hypothetical benchmark charts of the above variables. The vertical axis serves both for number of jobs (1 = 100) and investment (1 = $100,000). The horizontal axis is time in months. Relative to the vertical axis is a top curve benchmarking the number of jobs. The bottom curve benchmarks the amount of investment. In figure 9.2, it appears that although incubator investment varies somewhat, the benchmark curve for job creation is relatively flat, meaning no change in number of jobs. By contrast, figure 9.3 shows how a momentary boost in incubator investment initiates an upward increase across time of job creation. Note that this benchmarks a "lagged" effect—the boost in investment appears to initiate not just a momentary but an upward increase in job creation. The statistical method of time-series analysis[1] can be applied to test whether this is more than just a chance relationship across time. It will then serve as a benchmark of change—a valuable tool for evaluating investments as well as for planning. Benchmark studies are sophisticated tools for illustrating planning and evaluation for policymakers. After all, shouldn't objective data be used for evaluation where otherwise biased opinions might prevail?

NOTE

1. Frederick Williams and Peter Monge, *Reasoning with Statistics*, 5th ed. (Fort Worth: Texas Harcourt College Publishers, 2001).

CHAPTER 10

Technology Transfer

A new breeze is blowing across the world and is changing market systems within and among countries. Government and business leaders can no longer afford passively to regard the transfer of technology and its commercialization. They certainly can no longer take the technology-transfer process for granted. There are a large number of perplexing, often paradoxical and interrelated drivers that are forcing the rethinking, reshaping, and restructuring of technology transfer for domestic economic well-being, for global economic leadership, and for the future harmony of the world economy. In this chapter we spell out a strategy for change—a strategy where technology transfer is a key component.

IMPORTANCE OF TECHNOLOGICAL INNOVATION AND TRANSFER

Technology Exchange

In the United States, the current budget deficits and trade imbalances, rising capital needs, more demanding community expectations for economic development, and especially more intense international competition in global markets now require leaders to develop better and newer ways to transfer and commercialize science and technology. Economic relations among industrial countries in this decade have fallen into critical imbalance, while stagnation has become the lot of many developing countries. The drift that typifies current policies, if not corrected, could lead to a disaster from which none would escape.[1]

The concept of *technology exchange* is taking on a larger role. Those words now describe the process by which an entire nation harnesses its creativity and innovation in one realm—technology research—and translates that into leadership in a different realm: the competitive world of international business. Technology innovation is taking on an ever-increasing importance for setting our future domestic economic course as well as establishing the nature of U.S. world economic leadership. It is the process by which we go about harnessing our nation's R&D activities in science and technology and then transforming them into increased productivity for economic growth. It is the resulting economic growth that will help alleviate trade and budgetary deficits and economic problems facing this country as well as provide individual Americans with a higher real standard of living.

Factors of Technology Commercialization

Five important factors regarding the nature of technology and its commercialization in a modern economy have become clear:

1. Technology is a constantly replenishable national resource.
2. Technology generates wealth, which in turn is the key to economic, social, and political power.
3. Technology is a prime factor for domestic productivity and international competitiveness.
4. Technology is the driver for new alliances among academia, business, and government.
5. Technology requires a new managerial philosophy and practice.

Challenge to the Ever-Changing Economy

How can we manage technology creatively and innovatively to reap the benefits of sustained economic growth? Those who do so will play the key roles in resolving the paradox of global competition and cooperation. What is the nature of this paradox? How do we find ourselves in it today?

Particularly since World War II, technological innovation—the entire process, from R&D in the laboratory to successful commercialization in the marketplace—has been taken for granted. Traditionally, we have thought that the successful commercialization of R&D was the result of an automatic process that began with scientific research and then moved to development, financing, manufacturing, and marketing. Managers and administrators continually strove for excellent performance in their respective institutions. They did not necessarily need to be concerned with linkages in the technology-commercialization process. Insufficient attention was paid to the connections between the myriad institutions involved in moving scientific research from the laboratory to the marketplace. Most

thought that there was little practical need to be concerned with the connections among academic, business, and government leaders involved in
the commercialization process, in terms of understanding and evaluating
their institutional performance for a better society.

Today's Setting

The four-year study by the Office of Technology Assessment (OTA)
titled *Technology and the American Economic Transition: Choices for the Future*[2]
sets forth four major forces that are reshaping our society: (1) constantly
new emerging technologies, (2) the loss of U.S. preeminence in international markets, (3) the possibility that the price of energy and other natural
resources may increase sharply by the turn of the century, and (4) new
values and changing tastes among consumers.

The report stresses that technology is a major driver for transforming
the American economy in ways that are likely to reshape virtually every
product, science, and job in the United States.

The challenge posed by this important study is that the American economy is at a crossroads and its future rests on a set of conscious choices.
But do we really have a choice in pursuing leading-edge technologies?
One example is superconductivity. There is no question that innovation
in this technology will have an impact on a number of firms, industries,
products, and services and will affect the security of our nation. It is a
dual technology innovation having commercial and military applications.
There is little choice but to pursue a technological innovation with so
many significant ramifications. Yet, according to an article on the OTA
draft report in the *Wall Street Journal*, "Japanese companies are poised to
commercialize superconductivity technology well ahead of their U.S. ri-
vals, despite the U.S. lead in basic research." More than choice is involved
in the decision to pursue a technological innovation and its subsequent
successful commercialization. Successful commercialization involves the
ability to answer three key questions:

1. When and how to take leadership positions in science and technological innovations and their commercialization
2. How to play catch up when others have manufacturing and market leadership
3. How to leapfrog competition to become pertinent both scientifically and
   economically

Leaders in government, academia, and business have made it clear that
past policies, theories, doctrines, and practices are no longer adequate to
address these types of choices wisely. Peter F. Drucker[3] forcefully stated
that the world economy already has changed irreversibly in its foundations and structures: "It may be a long time before economic theorists

accept that there have been fundamental changes, and longer still before they adapt theories to account for them." The noted scholar on techno-logical innovation Dr. Ralph Landau[4] pointed out that technological change has been central to U.S. economic growth, both directly (in which case it can be said to count for perhaps 30% of economic growth) and through its positive effect on other factors of production (which can be said to account for perhaps another 40% or 50% of economic growth). Although scholarly research has not provided conclusive evidence yet, it is in this broad sense that technological innovation is the key to viable strategies for future economic growth: it can raise the productivity of the economy at an accelerated rate.

Today, there is a major transformation underway in which all leaders need to rethink technology's role in economic change domestically and internationally. What does it mean to today's leadership to take viable strategies for stable economic growth? Maintaining global market com-petitiveness is requiring more and more heavy capital commitments to new, more risky, often large-scale technologies that require 5 to 10 years to implement successfully. Often these choices are "bet the company" or "bet a whole American-based industry" decisions. At the same time, the key to this country's great economic gains has been the speed with which bright innovators have recognized technology potentials and then used their know-how to exploit them. From a leadership perspective, rethink-ing technology innovation's role in economic change requires a restruc-turing of the way (1) science and technology are developed and transferred; (2) businesses are managed; and (3) rules, regulations, and incentives operate within the private and public sectors to use technology innovation in a timely manner.

Technology has provided a range of opportunities and challenges to all of our leaders in academia, business, and government. When viewed from an international perspective, the challenge to speed up our nation's re-thinking process becomes more imperative. Why is this so? Technology has reshaped the products, services, and jobs in all nations, not just the United States. The Japanese story is well known. Former USSR premier Mikhail Gorbachev's book *Perestroika*[5] sets forth what he calls "the think-ing for USSR and the world." In terms of technology, and the USSR's "goal to meet world technological standards," Gorbachev[6] states,

We decided to put a firm end to the "import scourge" as our economic executives call it. To these ends we are putting into operation the great potential of our science and mechanical engineering. . . .

We are launching target-oriented programs, prompting work collectives and economic and other scientists to work in a creative way, and have organized twenty-two intersectoral research and technological complexes headed by leading scientists. The CPSU Central Committee set a target unprecedented in the history of the Soviet industry, that of reaching in the next six to seven years world standards as regards major machinery, equipment, and instruments.

Understanding the Technology Commercialization Process

Commercialization is the process by which R&D results are transformed into the marketplace as products and services in a timely manner. It requires the active interchange of ideas and opinions that are both technological and market-oriented in nature. The commercialization process may benefit through increased scale of production, higher quality, and lower prices. Commercialization helps to define the educational and training requirements for present and emerging marketplaces. It can also be a major driving force that invigorates emerging industries and rejuvenates older industries.

The traditional and still current strategy in our nation for commercializing technology is that industrial laboratories concentrate on mission-oriented projects and universities confine themselves primarily to basic research and teaching. During the past decade, advocates for changing this strategy recognized gaps—namely, the loss of global markets, the hollowing out of our manufacturing plants and piecemeal collaborative efforts for research and development, joint ventures at home and abroad, the buying out of American firms, and the growth of foreign companies in the United States.

The use of technology as a resource traditionally has been perceived as an individual institution's choice and responsibility. Economic developments would flow from this process because of American ingenuity and our entrepreneurial spirit. It was expected that all regions of the United States would in time enjoy the benefits of this paradigm, in which new innovations from research were followed naturally by timely developments, commercialization, and diffusion.

This traditional paradigm—that science and technology naturally evolve into commercialization—has clearly become inadequate. In the emerging economy, it does not adequately (1) provide sufficient employment opportunities; (2) mitigate layoffs and plant closures; (3) maintain a strong, global, and comprehensive security position; (4) provide regional and local economic development; or (5) present growth opportunities across the board for basic and high-technology industries.

Since 1996, a new paradigm has been emerging to meet the aforementioned realities. It includes institutional developments involving academia, business, and government technology venturing. These developments seek to maintain our leadership in science and technology by accelerating the successful commercialization of innovation in a competitive environment. The underlying assumption in this paradigm for commercialization is that scientific- and technology-innovation leadership can result in industrial and product leadership if our scientific talents are concentrated on applications selected by those who could commercialize them.

Throughout America, most of the states are moving to aid the growth of high technology and to foster technological commercialization. They, rather than the federal government, have taken leadership roles through policy-development organizations, economic-growth initiatives, and corporate-university partnerships. Since 1980, hundreds of programs or initiatives have been developed by states for high technology and economic development. For most states, the major source of R&D funds is still the federal government. There is a direct correlation between those states receiving the largest federal obligations for R&D and those taking the lead to initiate technology-venturing developments.

As a result, these activities are bringing together in dynamic and interactive ways state governments, local governments, private corporations, universities, nonprofit foundations, and other organizations. They are developing corridors and triangles between key cities or research universities. Centers of excellence are appearing within these corridors and triangles. They have begun to lay out science and research parks and target emerging industries for long-term industrial growth. Leadership networks are forming between previously isolated institutions. These developments are not accidental. These new institutional developments are managed efforts for economic growth and diversification that (1) develop emerging industries, (2) provide seed capital for early and start-up entrepreneurial endeavors, and (3) assure U.S. scientific/economic preeminence.

Developing Emerging Industries

The institutional relationships involved here are academic and industrial collaborations and industrial R&D consortia. Because the basic research is carried out in universities and colleges, collaborative efforts between academia and industry can accelerate the commercialization of basic research into emerging industries.

Since 1982, there have been a series of private-corporation joint-research efforts. The obstacle to such consortia in the past has been ambiguous legal status under the antitrust laws that would entail the risk of huge penalties. The passage of the Cooperative Research and Development Act in October 1984 has done much to alleviate these legal concerns. As a result of the passage of this act, there has been a proliferation of large-scale R&D consortia, which now number more than 150 nationwide.

Some forms of institutional development, such as incubators, SBIR programs, state venture-capital funds, and risk-capital networks, are providing seed capital for small and take-off companies. They are also pushing regional and local economic diversification through entrepreneurial activities.

Some states now are developing special initiatives such as tax incentives, enterprise zones, research and industrial parks, and direct financial assistance in the form of low-interest bank loans and loan guarantees to meet the start-up capital needs of new technology firms.

Assuring U.S. Scientific/Economic Preeminence

A number of institutional developments are seeking to ensure U.S. scientific and economic preeminence. The focus on the creation of National Science Foundation (NSF) centers of research and engineering excellence, government/business/university collaborative arrangements in technological areas, industrial R&D joint ventures and consortia, and the NSF's sponsorship of Industry/University Cooperative Research Centers were intended to provide a broad-based research program that would be too large for any one company to undertake alone.

Scholars and practitioners are reassessing the entire nature and direction of technology innovation and its commercialization. They are raising important questions about its effectiveness, theory, and direction. As a result, we find ourselves in a diverse and lively muddling process, trying to better understand the key factors involved in technology commercialization. On a variety of fronts, there are challenges on how we organize for and take advantage of technological innovation in a period of hyper-competition. For example:

- "Intellectually, there is a major problem to be sorted out. There is a powerful historical tendency for late comers to catch up with early comers."[7]

- "The ideal of the entrepreneur has been taken to excess . . . the constant spawning of new companies may be actually sapping America's economic might."

- Consortia members "will then 'compete away' part of the returns. . . . To that extent, none of the members will benefit."

- Setting priorities on science has been "a subject heretofore considered inappropriate for mention in polite scientific society. The question remains as to how this is to be done."

- "Our report makes one principal recommendation: Universities and corporations need to assess the results of their collaborative research and technology exchange efforts more systematically and effectively. This recommendation is offered in the conviction that the results of such assessments will further simulate productive cooperation."

- "A strong science base supplies a vast storehouse of new ideas, and a good educational system provides engineers and manufacturing workers with knowledge; but strength here cannot make up for inadequacies in the functioning of the development and manufacturing cycle."

It is apparent that we lack the necessary integration for successful technology commercialization. The requirements for developing such an integration in the coming economy demand the simultaneous linking of several factors:

1. **Need:** Is there motivation for pride, security, and profit?
2. **Vision:** Are there adequate mentors to foster creative collaborative programs?
3. **Timing:** Is there a real, current market need?
4. **Technical feasibility:** Does the technology exist? Is the required research underway?
5. **Skilled personnel:** Is there sufficient quality and quantity?
6. **Champions:** Is leadership available and in place?
7. **Adequate financial resources:** Has the necessary capital been committed?
8. **Public and political support:** Is there a consensus on key public-policy issues? How will it be sustained?
9. **Public-private sector cooperation:** Are the institutional alliances viable and effective?
10. **Intellectual community support:** Is the theoretical basis being developed in harmony with the new reality?

Successful technology commercialization usually takes longer and costs more than anticipated, and failures surely will occur along the way. Consequently, there must be contingency planning to incorporate the following needs:

1. Continuity of public and private support
2. Capital infusion
3. Parallel developments to alternative approaches and supporting technology
4. More skilled personnel than originally planned
5. The need for three types of leaders: one to start, another to move forward, and still another to take it to the marketplace

The relationship between technology innovation and economic wealth generation, resource development, markets, and job creation involves more than making economical investments. Just as important as the usual economic standards of effectiveness and efficiency are two other dimensions. First, flexibility: If we do not make the investments, will we still have sufficient flexibility to meet competitive challenges? Second, adaptability: If we do not make these investments, can we adapt ourselves to unexpected or unforeseen competition without serious consequences to our firms and communities? These are the challenges—flexibility and adaptability—that technology innovation poses.

Rethinking, Reshaping, and Restructuring for the Coming Economy

Meeting these challenges requires that we rethink, reshape, and restructure our approach to technology innovation for the coming economy. Rethinking will lead to a better definition of the technology-innovation process that, in turn, will influence national policy, industry development, and firm activity. Reshaping will lead to a more effective model of the economy that reflects the importance of networking and will help delineate alternative approaches to technology innovation. Restructuring will form the foundation for the new industries emerging from leading-edge technologies.

Multiple Challenges

The technology-innovation process requires a kind of parallel processing; many things have to be going on at the same time at many places. Technology innovation is not a clear-cut, step-by-step process. Linking R&D to the marketplace seems to most people to be a chaotic, complex, convoluted, and very messy process. But there is a connective pattern to this chaos. The pattern is a parallel one; actions need to be taken simultaneously in myriad institutions to move the technology to the market continually.

There is also a serious process at work at each nodal point of the movement of a technology from the laboratory to the marketplace. Some matters have to be done serially, such as individual projects. But each of these serial operations can, in many cases, be going on simultaneously. To illustrate this point, three examples follow: one at the national policy level, another at the industry level, and a third at the company level.

At the national level, the Japanese approach is interesting. It promotes many functions—like the following six, all of which have serial components but all of which are carried on in parallel:

1. International research cooperation
   a. Specific international joint-research projects
   b. Summit projects (e.g., Human Frontier Science Program)
   c. Invitation of foreign researchers to Japan
   d. Collaboration with developing countries in joint research projects
2. Technological development programs
   a. R&D basic technologies for future industries
   b. Large-scale projects
   c. R&D project for medical and welfare equipment
   d. Energy-related technologies

3. Regional economics
   a. R&D on important regional technologies
   b. Technopoleis program
   c. Joint government–private sector research

4. Promotion of technology development in the private sector
   a. Japan Key Technology Center
   b. Conditional loans for the development of technologies to activate industry in basic materials and core and priority technologies and to innovative basic technologies, environmental-protection safety technologies, regional technologies, and energy-conservation, power-generation, and oil-substitute technologies

5. Promotion of industrial standardization
   a. Voluntary standards for quality assurance and interchangeability of products for both domestic and foreign manufacturers
   b. Research for standards for material, textile and chemicals, machinery, electrical and electronic, and information standards
   c. Participation in international standardization

6. Diffusion of technology accomplishments
   a. Patents and licensing of state-owned intellectual properties
   b. International exchanges of technology

At an industry level, Debra Rogers[8] has described the parallel approach as "the process by which an entire nation harnesses its creativity and innovation in one realm—technology research—and translates that into leadership in a different realm—the competitive world of international business." Her technology-transfer continuum is an effective representation of this parallelism with its multiple feedback processes. She further describes the infrastructure for the commercialization of technology at an industry level in terms of structure, resources, and methods and tools available. The process itself is parallel. It is stimulated by creativity and implemented successfully through innovation, with parallel processing being coordinated through three institutions: education, government, and industry.

At a firm or company level, IBM is concerned with commercializing technology innovation as a two-step process with strong connections between development and manufacturing cycles. The first step is when a creative idea or technology dominates and is innovatively implemented in a specific product. The second step involves cyclic development or repeated incremental improvement to the product engineered by the first process. The repeated incremental advances result in product improvement with new features year after year. Although the process is evolutionary, the cumulative effects are profound in terms of market domination. As R. E. Gomory and R. W. Schmitt have pointed out: "In technology areas where the United States has not been competitive, we have lost, usually not to radical new technology, but to better refinements, better manufacturing technology, or better quality in an existing product." Consequently, it is important to develop a parallel process within the firm. Then, when a product is in the manufacturing stage, it is possible to have the development team working on the next creative idea or technology.

Professor Laura Tyson of the University of California at Berkeley was correct when she stated, "Simply put, in the long run, investment in science, education, technological innovation and technology diffusion is all that will sustain us." The challenge we face in making these investments is how we balance individual choices as investors, voters, consumers, and employers with institutional choices that affect the nature and scope of our nation's economic future. Reshaping our economy based on individual choices and connecting them to the requisite investments in science and technology is a difficult task. It is confounded further when we try to link these investments and their utilization with the myriad of institutions involved.

The American emphasis has been on individual capabilities. In this sense, Americans excel, according to Professor Iwao Nakatani, professor of economics at Osaka University:

A close look at those industries in which U.S. firms are competitive reveals that most belong to fields which attach little importance to coordination between people and offices, with success or failure usually hinging on the effective use of individual capabilities. This category would include such activities as basic research at universities and research institutes, the design of systems and software for computers, research and development of pharmaceuticals and aerospace industries such as missiles and aircraft. In these fields, individual creativity is crucial, while coordination does not hold much weight. These two factors are essential conditions for any industry in which the United States is to remain competitive.

In assembly and processing industries, however, a wide variety of parts are brought together from numerous suppliers and assembled through precise operations. This requires close links between people and organizations, as well as careful coordination of activities. Ordinary, day-to-day innovations generated in these relationships and interactions thus determine the competitiveness of the industry. These are precisely the industries in which the United States is having the most difficulties.

Overall, it could be concluded that the United States will hold onto its competitive edge in those industries in which individual ability is the prime criteria for success. In industrial sectors that stress coordination, however, it will be difficult for the United States to regain competitiveness even if the dollar plunges further.

It is imperative that the United States and Japan join hands to complement each other's weak points. While the strength of Japanese firms in terms of coordination is beyond question, they cannot even come close to matching their U.S. counterparts in making effective use of individual capabilities. U.S. corporations, for their part, generally experience great difficulty with "horizontal relationships," and could perhaps learn a great deal from the patience that characterizes Japanese corporate management. What is required of U.S. and Japanese corporations is not mutual hostility, but rather mutual cooperation.

Reshaping the U.S. Economy

Change in the American economy requires a framework to help chart its future direction—a direction that is being influenced by the result of myriad individual private choices; by the way businesses are being managed by rules, regulations, and incentives being adopted by the public sector; and by the use of emerging technologies. Since the first industrial revolution, technology innovation has been a basic motor for economic growth and job creation. For example, much of our economic growth in the past decade and a half has been influenced by information-technology innovations, coupled with job creation through small business firms.

By 1983 more than 50 percent of the U.S. GNP was derived from information technologies. Small business establishments generated 62 percent of the net employment increase between 1974 and 1984. Reshaping our approach to technology innovation must reflect the new realities of internationalization, interdependence, and networking. The OTA study[9] has set forth basic characteristics of the future American economy that effectively reflect these important themes:

1. Each part of the economy is interdependent with the other, forming a conceptual network.

2. Technology can increase the efficiency of the whole network and each part of the network.

3. Technology can greatly increase the efficient use of energy and materials if investments are made for the design of the parts and their management.

4. Problems in one part of the economy quickly impact on many other parts both directly and indirectly.

5. New connections grow quickly between parts of the economy.

6. Many parts of the economy have become internationalized and move about the world with ease and speed, such as products, finance, and ideas.

7. As the connections become more complex and as things move in parallel, the role of transactional businesspeople and professionals grows as well as their costs.

8. Businesses are locating where they can find adequately skilled and trained personnel in sufficient quantity and where extensive networks of personal contact can be maintained.

9. Technology has changed the nature of work done at home and at work.

10. Successful adaptation of the new economy will require skills provided by a solid basic education.

Economic Connectivity

A paradox of all the above is that countries, establishments, communities, and individuals are finding themselves more tightly connected. Yet the networks allow more independence and choice. In particular, technology may tie production systems in different countries more closely together while nations become less and less dependent on imported supplies of energy, food, and manufactured products. In such situations, the movement of materials may have decreased while the strength of linkages moving information, technology, ideas, and capital equipment has increased.

Alternative Strategies for Keeping Up

We must aggressively reshape our use of technology innovation using alternative strategies such as the following:

- Continue to have study commissions with reported recommendations and hold symposia and conferences on the topic of technology innovation and its commercialization.
- Foster and speed up better research to understand more fully the impacts of technology innovation and to forecast their changes on emerging industries and economic growth.
- Hold a national congress on technology innovation with a focus on its parallel-processing dimension.
- Hold national conferences on technology entrepreneurship to discuss incentives and barriers to technology innovation in small companies.
- Convene an international commission to provide direction on the world economy and world policy.
- Keep the status quo, thus letting technology evolve and basing reactions on production needs, individual choices, and crises.

Moving Now

The new century is ripe for reshaping our approach to technology innovation. The world political leadership is undergoing rapid change. Russia, China, Japan, and the European Union have changing leadership. The next few years provide an unprecedented opportunity for the world community to address the issues, concerns, and paradoxes that surround technology innovation and commercialization. Particular needs to be addressed include reciprocity in technological exchanges; intellectual-property rights; early access to new products, processes, and equipment; foreign investments in other nations; and workforce requirements.

Restructuring

Emerging industries are those that will be developed by using the revolutionary technologies that only now are beginning to move from invention to innovation, such as lasers, new materials, biotechnology, international telecommunication networks, very large integrated circuits, medical instrumentation, superconductors, and breakthrough managerial methodologies. These technologies have the following four characteristics, as pointed out by W. W. Rostow:[10]

- They are so encompassing that no one country can dominate them completely.
- They are linked to areas of the basic sciences that also are undergoing revolutionary changes.
- They are immediately transferable to rapidly industrializing nations.
- They are key to leapfrogging for basic industries.

The emerging industries based on these technologies are being challenged across all dimensions, from scientific development to invention, innovation, and commercialization. These industries must rely on government and academia to help meet the scientific and technical challenges upon which their viability depends.

If we are to maintain U.S. preeminence in these emerging industries, we must find more effective ways to maintain a global competitive edge in these arenas. Maintaining political and economic manufacturing advantages requires that we begin to think and act in new ways to commercialize technological resources, wherever they may be.

If the United States is to meet the competitiveness challenge facing this country, then we must take more of a global view. It is necessary to recognize that there is more and more emphasis on locating the best possible places around the world, in both economic and political terms, to conduct R&D, manufacturing, marketing, and financial activities. There is also more and more emphasis on the world as a single marketplace, rather than one that is subdivided nationally or regionally. Yet it is best to describe natural reactions to this today as protectionist, intensely competitive, and at best muddled.

Global competitiveness focuses on developing global relationships for science and implementing cooperative and competitive strategies among trade partners and allies. Competitiveness and cooperation seem to be a paradox, but they actually are the cornerstones for a more effective U.S. strategy for commercialization.

Competition is the outcome of those national attributes that help individuals and firms to perform more effectively and efficiently. Consequently, it enhances the relative strength of companies, facilitates international trade, and adds to the world's quality of well-being. Cooperation among scientific and technological organizations can become an important source for emerging industries. Improved processes for commercialization, for example, require more effective interaction among federal labs, industrial labs, and universities.

Technological innovation in the coming economy demands an integrated, holistic approach that blends technological, managerial, scientific, socioeconomic, cultural, and political ramifications in an atmosphere of extreme time compression. This approach centers on new ways for government, business, labor, and academia to work together.

In all, the United States still has the world's most creative technology base, a stable political system, a world-class higher educational system for research and teaching, the world's largest market, and a large capital base. We have a tradition of entrepreneurship and a demonstrated ability to respond rapidly to severe crises. We have the resources and the know-how to compete globally, to cooperate with other key nations such as Japan in providing world economic leadership, and to meet the challenge of technological innovation in the coming economy. We need to make the best use of these resources in our preparation to compete in the coming economy.

TECHNOLOGY TRANSFER AS A COMMUNICATION PROCESS

Source-Destination Model

As the theme of their book *Technology Transfer: A Communication Perspective,*[11] Frederick Williams and David V. Gibson cast technology transfer into the traditional SOURCE →MESSAGE→DESTINATION communication model wherein technology transfer is the iterative movement of applied knowledge ("message") via one or more communication channels with its communicating agents—scientists, manufacturers, marketers, clients, or customers in the roles of "sources" and "destinations" being engaged in the communication, sharing, or diffusion of scientific and technological knowledge, or, in more general terms, the transfer of knowledge from the laboratory (source) to the manufacturer or commercializer (destination).

Levels of Involvement

Drawing from earlier work by Raymond Smilor and David Gibson, the authors also differentiate among three levels of involvement reflecting responsibilities in the transfer communication process:[12]

1. **Technology development:** This first level involves the responsibilities of scientists as communication sources to communicate results of their research (mes-

sage) in scientific reports, convention papers, and referred journals, as well as in reports to their sponsors or clients (destinations).

2. **Technology acceptance:** On this second level, there is a responsibility that destinations have to gain technical information (message) for commercialization and the scientists who can provide it.

3. **Technology application:** This third level refers to responsibility on the parts of those (destinations) pursuing commercialization of science and technology—that information (message) not just be gained, but that the information can be applied for commercialization and profit.

The basic SOURCE→MESSAGE→DESTINATION model is a valuable paradigm for analyzing the transfer process as involving individuals, organizations, or steps in the technology-commercialization cycle.

Serendipitous Communication

A brief anecdote that your coauthor (FW) calls "Kindergarten Telecom Encounter" illustrates how technology-transfer communication may often occur outside of formal channels. In the late 1980s, the Texas governor led the development of what was to become a state agency for economic development. At the time, I was just completing several major projects at the University of Texas studying uses of telecommunications for business development and thought the results might be of use to the new agency. Consequently, I sent the interim director a letter offering assistance in the area of telecommunications development and enclosed a copy of our major research report. After receiving no response or acknowledgment for several weeks, I re-sent the letter and made a follow-up telephone call. "Yes, your kind offer had been received," explained an underling in the fledgling agency, "but our director says we have no new needs for telephone service." In the meantime, one of my key research assistants on the telecommunications projects (whom I'll call "Eduardo"), a graduate student, had a chance encounter with a young lady professional who was just starting with the development group (whom I'll call "Ms. Rogers") while they both were enrolling their daughters in kindergarten. In sharing their current work experiences, Ms. Rogers expressed her amazement that Eduardo had conducted research in telecommunications business opportunities, because, as she explained, the agency had thought they should add telecommunications to their development projects. The positive conclusion to the story is that Eduardo and Ms. Rogers arranged for an agency briefing on telecom business opportunities that eventually, with the support of the Southwestern Bell Company, grew into a state-level conference on telecommunications and economic development. None of this would have happened if not for our oft-told "Kindergarten Telecom Encounter."

All things considered, technology transfer is not always easy communication, because of different organizations, backgrounds, motives, and opportunities to make the link. We have to add that experience has shown that sometimes businesspeople find we in universities are not the best of sources or destinations.

NOTES

1. J. K. Galbraith, W. W. Weintraub, and S. Weintraub, *Proposal for a High Level Report by an International Commission on the Future of the World Economy (World Maekawa Report)* (Austin: University of Texas at Austin, LBJ School of Public Affairs, 1988).

2. Office of Technology Assessment, *Technology and the American Economic Transition: Choices for the Future* (Washington, D.C.: U.S. Office of Technology Assessment, 1988).

3. Peter F. Drucker, "The Changed World Economy," *Foreign Affairs* 64, no. 5 (1986), p. 47.

4. Ralph Landau, "U.S. Economic Growth," *Scientific American* 258, no. 6 (1988), pp. 61–63.

5. Mikhail Gorbachev, *Perestroika: New Thinking for Our Country and the World* (New York: Harper & Row, 1987), p. 203.

6. Ibid., pp. 94–95.

7. W. W. Rostow, telephone conversation with author, 21 October 1988.

8. Debra Rogers, D. M. A., "Toward a National Campaign for Competitive Technology Transfer" (paper presented at the AAAS Annual Meeting, Boston, 1988), p. 1.

9. Office of Technology Assessment, *Technology.*

10. W. W. Rostow, "The Fourth Industrial Revolution and American Society: Some Reflections on the Past for the Future," in *Cooperation and Competition in the Global Economy: Issues and Strategies,* ed. A. Furino (Cambridge, Mass.: Ballinger, 1988), pp. 172–181.

11. Frederick Williams and David V. Gibson, eds., *Technology Transfer: A Communications Perspective* (Newbury Park, Calif.: Sage, 1990).

12. Ibid., p. 14.

CHAPTER 11

Designing Industrial Parks and Incubators

Cities, regions, or nations wishing to promote new or accelerated economic development or diversification using science and technology will do well to consider very active and highly visible creation of facilities and services such as are found in industrial parks, business incubators, or enterprise centers. We have concluded that the most successful of these have been key agents for change—that is, in doing businesses in new and different ways, modernizing management practices, as well as undertaking entirely new businesses. In this chapter we review examples of these initiatives, inviting the reader to consider the relevance to their local situations.

WHAT ARE THESE PARKS AND CENTERS?

Among the most frequent examples of economic-development programs are industrial parks and business incubators. The former are much more common and have been in use for many years, although they vary considerably in size and programs. Some are government-sponsored, some under private, for-profit initiative—but all are meant to attract, retain, or enhance business opportunities. Incubators are found more in high-tech developmental programs and are meant to assist fledgling companies. Other concepts to consider are entrepreneurial or business-services centers and location of a development office. Centers or offices, in contrast with parks or incubators, do not typically have companies on-site.

PROS AND CONS OF INDUSTRIAL PARKS

"Don't Ask Me about Our Industrial Park"

In our studies of economic development in the United States and abroad, an oft-found programmatic example has been the industrial park. To be realistic, we'll start with a negative example found in a small southern city whose representative would prefer it not to be identified in the story, so we'll just call it "Southville." In the 1960s, the idea of industrial parks gained momentum. Most involved a program of setting aside land, maybe constructing a few basic buildings for inexpensive rental, and bringing in ready-to-use utilities like power, water and sewer services, and telecommunications. Offering an industrial park was becoming viewed as a near necessity for any city or locale that wanted to promote development.

Such parks or services were on our check-off list of facilities field research into the economic development of small developing cities in the 1980s. In one, however, we touched upon a raw nerve in meeting with the local chamber of commerce, where we received the "wish you hadn't asked me" story.

They had jumped on the bandwagon, encouraged the local government to acquire currently vacant land near a railroad siding and secondary highway, and with some cooperation from local business leaders who saw themselves as possible partners of newly recruited companies, invested in a start-up infrastructure of inexpensive industrial buildings, utilities, and a tax-abatement program. It seemed like a timely package: A brochure and about 10 regional billboards called out, "The dynamic 'City of Southville' . . . wants you to grow with us. We have great cost breaks for you; a pleasant city and countryside for living and fine schools and even fine fishing." Initially they recruited about six small manufacturing firms, but the big coup, they thought, was a major company undertaking a recycling business, including used auto motor oil. The latter turned out to be one of the greatest problems: their oil handling was so sloppy that there was a threat to contaminate several local city wells. Although the tax-abatement package seemed modest (30% to 50% off of local rates for the first decade), it soon was evident that the 50 or so children of families moving to work in the park would have a visible cost impact on the local schools, who were indirectly contributing to the rebate program—a double whammy.

Two additional problems reared their heads in the first several years. One was that the company shortchanged their workers on benefits, which had not been closely examined in agreements. Almost immediately, the local hospital was faced with providing services that the company's health-insurance providers declined to reimburse at cost rates. Moreover, in the second year, about 10 employees were laid off for three months, which impacted local unemployment funds. The recycling company had been naive about potential revenue streams, their costs of operation, and an expected host of new environmental requirements laid down by federal and state governments. They failed in their seventh year, declaring bankruptcy and unable to pay many of their local suppliers. Lawsuits filed against the company owners on their personal estates got the workers paid some back wages, but all else was a disaster. The final embarrassment was that when the city decided about all they could do with the contaminated land was to add it to the city dump operation, new environmental regulations prevented them from doing even that. Like the chamber office said: "I wish you hadn't asked." "You can tell our story so some folks won't go out and make the same mistakes, but please don't tell them it happened here in our city."

On the Positive Side of Industrial Parks

Basic Characteristics

The following section lists services and positive characteristics of industrial parks we have noted over the years. You can use this check-off list to brainstorm your local application.

Industrial Park Characteristics

1. Physical plant
   - Land, security, space for building, existing buildings, shops, or administrative spaces to rent
2. Business-to-business (B2B) services
   - Access to broadband telecom, Internet, and Web services assistance
   - Availability of computing services
   - A commercialization or entrepreneurial center offering concepts, strategies, and services needed to make the leap from traditional to high-tech fast-company creation and management
   - Legal services, including expertise in licensing, regulation, and taxation
   - International consultation on markets, transportation, and regulations
   - Language translation, when applicable
   - Legal advice on patents, copyrights, and trademarks
   - Research capabilities of local college or university; relationship-building
   - Assistance in negotiating with likely suppliers (maybe a discount program)
   - Administrative services on-site or easy access such as for fax, phone, Internet, and computing
   - Meeting or conference facility on-site or nearby; videoconferencing capabilities
3. Financials
   - Cooperative commercial and consumer-oriented banking
   - Special or low-interest loan money
   - Grants

- Tax-abatement program
- Attractive cost of living

4. Human resources
   - Local educated workforce
   - Positive demographics for education, work experience, and special skills
   - Affordable (to company) wage environment
   - Cooperative unions, if area is unionized
   - Positive work ethics
   - Training available, on-site or at schools

5. Quality of life
   - Primary, intermediate, and high schools
   - Community college, especially one that could provide certain worker skills
   - Affordable housing, clean environment, and low crime
   - Easy transportation to and from work
   - Recreational amenities, parks, swimming, golf course, sports facilities, movie house, local live theater
   - Retail shopping (a mall, for example)
   - Hospital and outpatient care programs

6. Park layout
   As shown in figure 11.1 a prototype industrial park can offer the following:
   - Inexpensive, buildable land, maybe with some existing buildings or pads
   - Easy access to transportation: local roads, highways, rail siding, and maybe a waterway
   - Ready-to-use, affordable utilities like electricity, water, wastewater, and telecommunications
   - Storage and warehousing

7. Where's headquarters?
   Although most parks we've studied have a kind of head office on-site, there are several points to consider if you are planning or working with an industrial park. If the park is in the countryside, you may want to consider a main office located in a city where staff can freely mix with the business or government crowd—that is, near government, chamber, or related economic-program offices, including banks or even a university campus. Many important contacts are made serendipitously. Thus proximity between your development director or staff and individuals in government, a development agency, banks, or a university may be very beneficial. It makes planning meetings easier and facilitates serendipitous encounters. You don't want your developmental officers and staff too far isolated from the centers of decision and power. So you may wish to locate only those directors or supervisors at the park site who have hands-on responsibilities with your client companies.

8. Maybe a high-tech headquarters or office and not a park?
   We've seen successful developmental facilities concentrated in a single "smart" building. In such cases, a lot of space is not your key tool; it's technical services, expertise, and proximity to partners, like those found in a university, government offices, or nearby labs or R&D centers. A smart building has all the computing and telecom services immediately available at affordable prices.

Figure 11.1
Prototype Industrial Park. Offering (1) flexible manufacturing facilities ("shops") with installed access to dual power (electricity and gas), water, waste-water, and a local-area telecommunications network; (2) free-standing storage; (3) space in an administrative building that includes meeting rooms; and (4) an adjacent communications facility. The park offers 24-hour security meeting the highest standards, including badge-passport services. © 2003 George Kozmetsky and Frederick Williams.

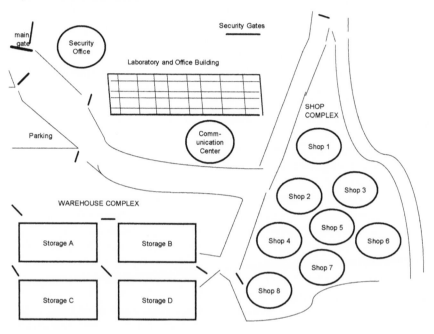

Example: Trinidad and Tobago Technology and Innovation Park t-Zone[1]

The t-Zone project represents an excellent example of contemporary high-tech development in a small nation. The country is a two-island nation in the West Indies off the coast of Venezuela. It has a strong economy dominated by petrochemicals, which they have wanted to diversify into tourism and high-tech industrial development. For the past five years they have sought to promote the latter by development of an advanced industrial park.

Currently, the t-Zone will be an 1,100-acre technology and light-industry park situated on a former U.S. airport at Wallerfield in eastern Trinidad and Tobago, 15 kilometers east of the Piarco International Airport and 20 kilometers east of the University of the West Indies St. Augustine Campus. The t-Zone will serve as a regional center for innovation, technology development, and application, seeking target tenant industries and companies in the following areas:

- Incubation and indigenous business development
- Call centers and back-office operations
- Software development
- Logistics services and light manufacturing
- Biotechnology/pharmaceuticals (research and manufacturing)
- Telecommunications equipment and other light manufactures
- Petrochemical-sector R&D
- Training
- High-tech conference facilities

Fiber-optic telecommunications facilities and electricity supplies will service all tenants, with redundancy built in where necessary. In addition, an adequate water supply and natural gas will be supplied to the site.

The site master plan and engineering designs for the t-Zone have been completed, and the project commenced in the fourth quarter of 2002 with the physical infrastructure development and active economic marketing stage. The first phase will provide access to 100 acres of the park for development. The construction of the 120,000-square-foot Technology Incubator and Commercialisation Centre will be within this 100-acre area. This center has already been programmed and will provide state-of-the-art office, lab, and manufacturing space to local and foreign businesses.

The t-Zone is being developed by the government of Trinidad and Tobago in collaboration with local industry and with the active support of the University of the West Indies and other tertiary education providers. Trinidad and Tobago has reliable and low-cost energy and an educated and highly trainable labor force. It is an eastern standard time zone nearshore location with modernized customs and export procedures and no foreign-exchange controls.

ABOUT INCUBATORS

Mission

Although their definitions vary, most business incubators aim to assist in starting and building companies. Because, as mentioned above, there is a major dependence on change and innovation for high-tech business development, incubators have become especially visible in the last several decades as catalysts for the development of businesses involving the commercialization of science and technology. Including high-tech and other firms, the National Business Incubator Association[2] counts upward of 900 incubator undertakings in the United States alone, up from only about a dozen in the 1980s. We do not have a count but have examined at least another three dozen internationally.

Essentially, incubators work to provide entrepreneurs and investors with the expertise, networks, and technologies they need to make their ventures successful. For economic-development programs, they can aid in business diversification, direct creation of jobs, and generation of wealth.

Austin Technology Incubator

Closest in our experience is the Austin Technology Incubator. As drawn from their descriptive materials: In June 1989, the University of Texas at Austin, through the IC[2] Institute and its then founder-director, Dr. George Kozmetsky, initiated a community-based experiment in launching companies devoted to science and technology. It was named the Austin Technology Incubator (ATI) and was led by founding ATI director Laura Kilcrease; funded by the University of Texas at Austin, the Greater Austin Chamber of Commerce, the city of Austin, Travis County, and private businesses; and advised by a committee of business professionals. ATI became a true consortium of academic, government, and business interests dedicated to building a technological business infrastructure in the Austin community.

From its inception, ATI has enjoyed wide support and success. Only two years after ATI's doors opened, Ms. Kilcrease was named the 1991 Austin Entrepreneur of the Year. In 1994, ATI was named the Randall M. Whaley Business Incubator of the Year. In 1995, ATI moved and now occupies approximately 45,000 square feet of office space in the prestigious MCC building in northwest Austin (3925 Braker Lane). The incubator has also expanded its reach into the Austin multimedia community (through the creation of the Austin Multimedia Incubator) and globally (through the creation of the Global Business Accelerator).

Over the last decade, ATI has facilitated the growth of over 95 companies; graduated more than 50 companies; and created over 1,900 direct, value-added jobs in Austin. ATI companies have produced revenues exceeding $700 million and have raised almost $200 million since originally bootstrapping themselves from an idea. This impressive growth added to the expanding technology base of the Austin area and fueled the local economy.

The current director of ATI is Dr. Joel Wiggins, a recently elected board member of the National Business Incubator Association.

IN CLOSING

As we said in the introduction to this chapter, doing any new business in science and technology requires change—new ways of doing business and the businesses that you do—so nearly any program offering assistance to the entrepreneur, investor, or development executive (whether it be start-up space, seed capital, training, consulting, networking, or just plain hand-holding) is worthy of consideration. Among the most valuable services we have observed are the following—as a kind of "final check."

- Offering informal, early, up-front advice (is there a business to be developed here?)
- Assistance in developing, final writing, and oral presentation of business plans
- Networking entrepreneurs with one another
- Networking entrepreneurs with investors
- Assistance with the legalities of getting started—local laws, licenses, and so on
- Holding workshops on innovations, know-how, and change
- Orienting the inventor, technical expert, and engineer to the challenges of markets and marketing
- Updates on practices, procedures, and laws regarding employment, workforce, benefits, and the demands for human-resource management
- Locating sources of information and setting up research projects
- Building a list of local or regional experts, consultants, or potential employees
- Introducing the new businessperson to others in the business community (lunches, seminars, social hours, etc.)
- Assistance with publicity, brochures, news releases, and relations with the media
- Introduction to local experts in nearby colleges or universities
- Assistance in locating important contacts or linkages in government—at every level from city to nation

Many of the above may seem overly obvious, but it is often these smaller considerations that can add up to, or discourage, success. Whether you are an investor, entrepreneur, or development executive, ask, what is your group doing in the way of parks, incubators, or enterprise centers?

NOTES

1. See http://www.techparktnt.com/. We are indebted to Mrs. Carl A. Francis and Kevin G. F. Stewart for this information.

2. The National Business Incubator Association (NBIA) is an excellent source of information not only on the status of incubators today, but on strategies for creating them. It is easiest to contact them via their Web site (http://www.nbia. org/), or at 20 East Circle Drive, Suite 190, Athens, Ohio 45701; tel: (740) 593-4331; fax: (740) 593-1996. They report roughly 1,200 members from 50 countries.

CHAPTER 12

Why an Enterprise Center?

Enterprise centers, like incubators, are a change agent but do not necessarily offer space and have resident firms, although they may work with the latter. What know-how, contacts, business plan analyses, market research, and sources of investment capital will assist entrepreneurs in getting started and growing their companies? In everyday talk, "How do you get the rubber to meet the road"—up and running? In this brief chapter, we offer our experiences in reviewing various types of enterprise centers and cite a few examples.

Four Reasons for Establishing an Enterprise Center

1. **Building new attitudes:** High-tech business development requires a lot of attitude change. We have many visitors who come to Austin to see, firsthand, high-tech businesses and catalyst organizations like the Austin Technology Incubator. Some go away enlightened and enthused; but some also seem to be in a state of denial from the very first experience of these new businesses and radical changes in ways of doing business. I (FW) recall one case where a very successful older businessman from a small nation accompanied his country's representatives who came to discuss development of an industrial park. Perhaps this man was just too successful in the old ways, which he constantly cited along with the very few questions he asked during the day's tour. (I fear the only question we answered successfully was where to mail the postcards he had been so busy writing during our presentations!) Making a commitment to, and following up with, aggressive operation of an enterprise center will help change attitudes in the desired direction.

2. **Managerial and corporate learning:** We're talking about personal as well as organizational learning, including using the kinds of tools described in part III.

An enterprise center can be a teaching process where the mission is to make efficient the technology transfer of organizing and managing the fast companies; it can be a learning hub where entrepreneurs, investors, new managers, and developmental planners come together.

3. **Concept evaluation and procedural advice:** Citizens or entrepreneurs who come up with ideas for new businesses are often limited on where they can go for evaluation of their ideas and knowledgeable advice for proceeding.

4. **Commercial forum or meeting place:** So often in this book we stress the importance of cooperation and partnerships among business and developmental stakeholders. Simply as a meeting facility or an organization offering a regular schedule of business-development events, workshops, summits, and speakers.

A FEW EXAMPLES OF ENTERPRISE CENTERS

Entrepreneurial Centre, Kingston, Jamaica

Many of the services other than residency, space, and the like, already listed in chapter 11, could be an offering of an enterprise center or institute. At the University of Technology in Jamaica, they have established the Entrepreneurial Centre, specifically designed to assist new companies, especially in information or overall technology businesses. From their Web site announcement, the center aims "to create efficient, profitable and innovative organizations promoting entrepreneurship through the provision of education, training and business support services of the highest quality; serving the University of Technology, Jamaica community, private companies and individuals in Jamaica and the Caribbean, with the aim of increasing sustainable economic activity in the nation and the Caribbean region as a whole."

The Enterprise Center (Philadelphia)

Founded by the Wharton School in 1989, the Enterprise Center "recruits, trains, and nurtures entrepreneurs and grows start-up companies in urban communities." They promote the belief "that the entrepreneurial spirit is the keystone of community growth and revival."

Enterprise Center of Johnson County (Kansas)

"Our Mission: to stimulate business creation and employment in Johnson County by providing value-added resources and services to early stage, high growth-oriented companies."

In closing this chapter, we strongly urge that any industrial park that has not already planned an enterprise center or office component consider one, lest they miss the learning curve of technological change and populate themselves with "sunset" rather than "sunrise" industries. Also, establishing and operating an enterprise center is a worthy undertaking for a university or a business college, since it is essentially a knowledge or know-how service. Being able to envision transitions to high-tech products and services, designing and operating a fast company, and understanding the Zero Time concept takes rapid learning and adjustment. It takes time and experiences to overcome old habits and stereotypes. If you are selecting partners or even consultants for an enterprise-development project, have a return look at the characteristics of adopters as compared with laggards, described in chapter 9.

PART III

Advances in Management Science

CHAPTER 13

Enhancements in Applied Research

"If you cannot measure it, you do not know what you are talking about"—so said Lord Kelvin, brilliant British physicist of the nineteenth century and designer of the first transatlantic telecom cable. In today's high-tech world, entrepreneurs and economic-development specialists now have at their hands powerful new research tools for evaluating the results of their business-improvement efforts and to feed forward those results to assist in further business development or enhancement, as well as economic development, proposals for new projects, or policymaking. Added to these are enhanced business research tools for decision and risk analysis, including assistance programs that run on desktop or laptop computers. All these tools for applied research give us not only bases for drawing data-based generalizations, but provide a common language and set of assumptions so we can communicate these generalizations clearly and effectively. This chapter reviews applied tools for practical use in business and economic development, especially as involving science and technology in rapidly changing situations, or what we call the *fast company* (chapter 5). Chapter 14 presents overviews of decision and risk analyses. We conclude with comments that distinguish the character of applied research from theoretical research. The organization of the present chapter is as follows:

- A Note on Research
- Research Methods
- Measures
- Statistics You Can Use

- A Few Representative Research Models
- Who Does the Statistics?
- Contrasts with Theoretical Research

A NOTE ON RESEARCH

Practically speaking, *research* refers to having a practical plan for study-ing or assessing something. It can be quite informal, as in setting about to interview, say, customers about their next year's needs and wishes, or reactions to your existing products or services. You'll probably be aware at the outset that your questions ought to be consistent, getting at the kinds of answers you can reliably use, and if different helpers are doing the study, they ask the same questions in the same way. Similarly, you'll want some consistent method for recording responses—say, open-ended notes, a multiple-choice list, or maybe even some type of scale to check off. Much of this is just plain common sense, and if whatever you write up about the study stresses the consistency of asking questions and re-cording the answers, others who eventually read the study will have more confidence in it. At this point, we ought to face up to the word *science* as you may hear it applied in business or economics research. Practically speaking, if you are told a piece of research—for example, a study of new business opportunities or development in some city or nation—is *scientific*, it asserts that a formal research method, typically recognized in the field, has been employed, and may further connote that the study relates to, draws from, or contributes to an existing body of generalizations or theory on the topic. Now, we purposefully contrasted the terms *assert* and *connote* in the foregoing statement to make the point that a methodological claim may be more straightforward and believable when one says that a study is scientific, as contrasted with any implication that they are dealing in a recognized and formal manner with theory, which among other scientists or researchers could be debatable within the give-and-take of that body of theory. We'll return to more comments on theory at the end of this chapter, but for now the relevance of science to method is important to our discussion. As research becomes more formal, it may become more scientific in a methodological sense as the consistency quality is carried out in the selection and implementation of your study method. In the social sciences one soon encounters several sets of distinctions when it comes to talking about method—for example, descriptive versus experi-mental methods, and qualitative versus quantitative methods.

RESEARCH METHODS

Descriptive versus Experimental Studies

A descriptive study is where you study things *as is*, as contrasted with conducting an *experiment*, where you manipulate the situation in some manner with the anticipation of observing effects and possibly drawing a cause-and-effect conclusion. Population and business census studies are descriptive research, as is the customer survey we mentioned above. As an example of an experiment, suppose that you wanted to test a new Web site to determine whether it interested your customers in one of your new product lines. You could set up that Web site where it would not likely be seen unless you directed a customer's attention to it. Suppose you selected 100 of your representative customers, then randomly picked 50 of them to be sent an invitation to the new Web site (your *experimental* group); another 50 might get an invitation to examine something in another of your existing Web sites (with no new products shown—your *control* group). After sufficient time for both groups to respond to your invitations, you then do an e-mail or telephone survey asking about interest in any new products. If all goes according to your expectations, you'd expect that the experimental group would have more new product interests than the control group. Now, as obvious as this may sound, you do have the basis, through the simple experimental design, to draw a cause-effect conclusion. If these were similar customers to begin with, and their only difference was seeing the new Web site, any expressions of new product interest can be reasonably attributed to the new site. (Note that we were careful to invite both groups to view something and to contact them both later, so just getting this attention could not make the difference.)[1] If there are no differences, you have a problem; either the message does not get across, or they have no new needs they wish to express. Where you do find effects, you can study them further, maybe in follow-up interviews. At some point, you could test cost figures in a companion experiment—how much investment in a Web site brings how much desired response from customers, and did the customer later buy? Today's cross- and mixed-media campaigns (Internet plus traditional media, including calling and mailing) offer many opportunities for applied research to assist in fine-tuning your best options and cost-per-customer of your marketing.

Qualitative versus Quantitative Methods

In research methods we speak of *data* (singular *datum*) as the information gathered in the course of a study. Some practical studies, like the example we just gave, are obvious mixes of qualitative (people's names, demographics, products, etc) and quantitative data, the latter being when we use numbers for description, often referring to measures. Typically one talks about measuring *variables*, any phenomenon—like age, annual salary, skill-test score, years of service, or the rated level on some scale of a particular occupation—where a numerical description has useful meaning. Sometimes in studies we are interested in whether the presence or absence of a variable makes any difference; we call this approach the use of *dummy* or *binary* variables, where its presence could be signified by the number 1 and its absence by the number 0—for example, whether workers have had training (1) or not (0).

MEASURES

Numerical Data

Numerical data can mean many things: *enumeration* (e.g., 50 customers, $18,000, etc.); *ordinal,* or the order of things (1st, 2nd, 30th, etc.); the location on a defined *interval* scale or range of numbers at intervals signifying more or less of something (her IQ is 120; my grade point average is 3.2; on a scale from 1 to 10, I'd give the president a 5 for leadership); or a so-called ratio, or absolute scale, where there is a true zero point (zero degrees Kelvin is where there is no molecular, or heat, activity). We also have categorical measurement, or a *nominal* scale, where data involve putting observations into fixed categories having no denotation about numerical differences other than the frequency of items in them—for example, blue, black, brown, or green eyes; Republican, Democrat, or independent; male or female; African American, Hispanic, or Anglo; and so on. Sometimes the various types of measurement are differentiated as levels, some providing more descriptive detail than others:

1. Ratio
2. Interval
3. Ordinal
4. Categorical

Although you surely want the scale that fits what you think you are talking about, a general preference is to use the most powerful one that can be related to your study. Also, only ratio and interval scales use numbers in ways that can legitimately employ the rules of arithmetic, although many applications ignore this restriction because the consequences are not all that disastrous. It is important to be realistic; numbers can mean a lot of things. What do your numbers describe, what is their quality, what is their level of measurement, and how are they assigned?

There's the story of the restaurant customer whose Chinese fortune cookie had a slip with "666" on it, and after the waitress ran off screaming, he went from table to table asking what it meant. Looking up from his soup, a mathematician said it was the square root of 443,556. An oil-company man said he thought it was the name of an old gas station. A young bearded man who was doing the restaurant Web site explained that it was a north-south highway somewhere in the southwest off of

I-10. A helpful rabbi said to look in the Bible's Book of Revelation. A psychologist said it could mean anything that would make him feel good. A bespectacled accountant said he couldn't help because he was on parole. An evil-looking gent holding a pitchfork under his table said, "You don't really want to know—beastly story!"

On the serious side, numbers can denote about anything we define for them—a name, an enumeration, or a scale of some type as described above. In the main, we look for *validity* and *reliability* in our measures. Validity means that you are describing what you claim to be measuring. Are the inches on the ruler accurate? Will they match a standard? Reliability means consistency of measurement: if repeated under exact conditions, will a measure show the same results? Validity implies reliability, but not vice versa. The ruler could be misprinted with the wrong size inches, but would show the same reading every time.

STATISTICS YOU CAN USE

Definition

The term *statistics* has multiple meanings—in an overall use; in a branch of applied mathematics; but, more specifically, in individual applications, models, formulas, or concepts for describing arrays of numbers, the larger population they may represent, or probabilities that certain numbers, ratios, and so on may occur or distribute if you have randomly sampled observations.

Descriptive Statistics

Some statistical models assist us in describing a frequency distribution of measures; following are several examples.

Means and Variance

A very common statistic is the *arithmetic mean.* We use the formula for an arithmetic mean to calculate the average in an array of measures or scores, or we can calculate an estimate of score dispersion called *variance.* Items like means and variances are themselves referred to as *statistics,* or *descriptive statistics*—characteristics of a distribution of numbers.

Correlation

There are many measures that *vary together*—that is, as one increases, the other increases or decreases. For example, people's height and weight tend to be correlated. Taller people tend to weigh more than shorter ones, a positive correlation, although, of course, there are exceptions. The older your automobile, the less it is probably worth—a negative or inverse correlation—unless you have preserved a valuable antique classic auto, an exception. A statistical model called *product-moment correlation* allows you to take two sets of measures on the same phenomena or replicates and calculate a coefficient of correlation, symbolized by an italicized *r*. Perfect positive correlation, when one variable always increases in a value with increases in another, is an *r* of +1.0. The opposite is an *r* of −1.0, when an increase in the value of one variable is accompanied by a decrease in the other. An *r* of 0, or a small one that might occur just out of chance, is interpreted as no relation or correlation. Although cause-effect relations (e.g., caloric intake of food and gaining weight) show a correlation, there are many correlations that do not represent cause and effect—for example, time of day and the rising or falling of the tide.

Population and Probability Statistics

The practice of statistics also provides us with mathematical models *(population statistics)* showing the probability characteristics of the greater population from which our scores are assumed to be gathered. Here, population reflects any of the greater universe of some phenomenon—not necessarily people; it could be light bulbs or tulips—having a numerical distribution of some trait. This is a reflection of the fundamental premise that if numbers, measures, or scores are gathered (sampled) randomly from a larger population, their frequency distribution will form a bell-shaped or so-called normal curve. The normal curve not only shows the frequency with which we have obtained certain scores, but also has its own characteristics. It is divided at its average, or population mean, by baseline units called *deviations*; taking the area under the curve as equal to 1.0, half of the scores will fall either above or below the mean point, and within these, .34 of them out one deviation above or below the mean, and so on, as you can see in the figure. After we estimate what these deviation units are equal to in terms of our numbers *(standard deviation, or sigmas)*, we can make probability estimates of certain scores occurring. For example, in figure 13.1 there's a .68 probability that we will have scores between 44 and 52, or .042 below 40 or above 56. This is just a taste of how the normal curve, as related to a distribution of measures, can be used to estimate probabilities. We use it to estimate the confidence we have in certain scores or statistical estimates, or, more valuable yet, the test of hypotheses about whether one or several distributions of scores could come by chance from the same population. As in the simple experiment described earlier, we could ask in terms of measures whether the customers who viewed the Web site message were from a different population from those who did not. We can estimate the probability that the difference in scores could have occurred by chance. If that probability turns out to be low—like under .05—we would reject a hypothesis of no difference and accept the alternative that our experiment changed customers. You've probably already read in articles or reports about rejecting a null hypothesis at the $p < .05$ (probability less than .05) or .01 level; that's what this is all about, and you can do a lot with it in research as a planner or manager. Some examples follow.

A FEW REPRESENTATIVE RESEARCH MODELS

An Experiment with Test of Differences

For an example, let us return to the sample experiment described earlier where customers were referred to a Web site promoting new products. As an experimental model, as illustrated in figure 13.1, there was an *independent* variable having two conditions: (1) the *experimental* group, selected at random, was invited to view a Web site promoting new products, whereas (2) the *control* group, also randomly selected, saw a site with no such promotion. The outcome, or *dependent* variable, was a count of the number of new products customers mentioned when called about having viewed the Web site. We could set up a statistical test of differences in the mean scores of the two groups, saying that if the probability of the difference we have observed would only be estimated to occur in 5 out of 100 cases of random sampling, a null hypothesis of no difference can be rejected at a chosen probability level (e.g., $p < .05$), and its logical alternative (our research hypothesis) would be accepted.

A Descriptive Study Using Correlation and Regression Models

Enterprise-Center Model

Again, unlike the above experiment, in descriptive studies you are studying some differences or relationships or sometimes making predictions about variables. Following is a hypothetical example of the use of correlation and regression to evaluate the development and operation of an enterprise-services center. This is the type of business-services organization used to assist new or updated business creation as well as a tool for economic development.

The Study

Researching the component operations of such a center can not only evaluate its operation (Are you getting a return on the investment? What's giving you the best returns?) but can evaluate it as a design strategy for setting up new organizations at other sites or contexts. Figure 13.2 illustrates the component operations of a successful enterprise center where, as a descriptive study, you are studying them as is rather than manipu-

Figure 13.1
Model for a Sample Experiment.

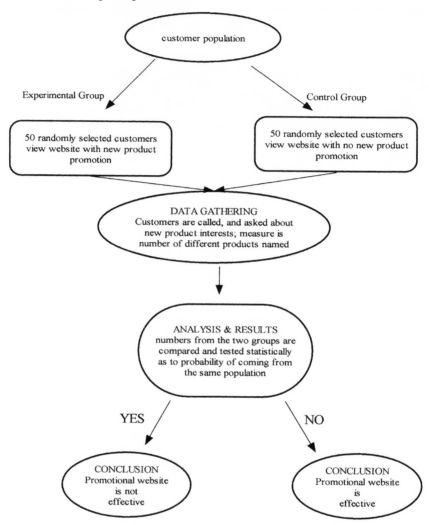

lating or controlling them for an experiment. We have called it the Maintown Enterprise Service Center.

Components Model

Figure 13.3 shows the main components for the center, including the design team, notes on financial loans, grants, venture capital, tax abatement, and so on. Some components are more critical for start-up than

Figure 13.2
Correlation-Regression Model. Hypothetical example for evaluating an enterprise services center.

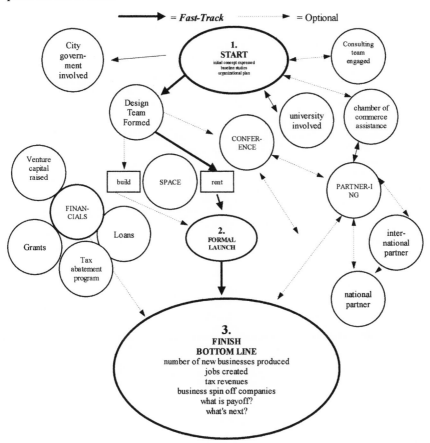

others. In fact, in laying out the chart, we are reminded that there is a potential "fast path" for getting underway. Note the three key steps: (1) *start*, (2) *formal launch*, and (3) *finish*, or *bottom line* (business revenues generated, jobs created, etc.). The dark line and arrow show a fast-track start-up option. Among other features, the path gets underway right with the design team; it skips a developmental conference and goes on to plan early rental of space while maybe putting off construction. This can eventually be compared with a more normal time operation, or even one that allows for delays (lagged) where there might be benefits (more time for construction bids, no overtime construction labor, extra time to recruit client companies, etc.). Among the disadvantages of the fast-track option are that early acquisition and cost of rental space is required unless the

city or some benefactors lend or donate space, which does happen occa-
sionally in development projects. We'll say for now that this started with
three planning alternatives that could be researched and eventually evaluated or examined in a decision model (chapter 14). In summary, the three
alternatives are as follows:

1. **Fast-track:** Try to be ready for service to 10 companies within one year. It may
   mean extra costs due to speeding up the bidding process, spending on
   construction-labor overtime in order to meet the schedule, and rent on a tem-
   porary building.
2. **Normal:** Take the usual amount of time for projects of this nature, which may
   mean about two to two and a half years until companies can be serviced. There
   could be savings in construction cost, avoidance of rent, and more time to recruit initial clients.
3. **Lagged:** Proceed in a normal fashion, but when some time out is of advantage,
   take it. Ask the constructor to discount for no time penalties or extra time for
   constriction. Use extra time for added recruitment of early clients. Maybe take
   early time to have a planning conference or recruit some local, national, or
   international partners.

Research Question

Suppose, for a descriptive-study example, we wished to evaluate the
relative relationships of these components with the bottom line, or payoff
of the project in business activity or related values. We could examine
these relations in terms of their costs or for some components, like a conference, whether we had one or not. To keep the example simple, let us
consider asking about the relative relations of the costs of component-
operation variables with a bottom line or outcome variable of creating an
observed level of business activity—say, average weekly revenue income
jobs.

Correlation Calculation

Recalling that a coefficient of correlation varies between $+1.0$ (perfect
positive correlation), 0 (no correlation), and -1.0 (perfect inverse or negative correlation), have a look at table 13.1, which shows some sample
correlations that might be found in this analysis.

Interpretations

The key results in table 13.1 are correlations of the component variables.
Calculated indexes are not usually at the extremes; we interpret them in
a relative sense. For example, the program components most related to
bottom-line results are the tax-abatement and venture-capital variables,
followed by government investment in the center program. Irrelevant was

Table 13.1
Sample Correlations

VARIABLES	1	2	3	4	5	6	7	8	9	10
1. government	1.00	0.66	0.08	0.20	0.70	0.10	0.00	0.05	0.78	0.67
2. venture cap.		1.00	0.40	0.06	0.09	0.40	0.78	0.30	0.88	0.88
3. university			1.00	0.69	0.14	0.46	0.23	0.88	0.05	0.60
4. conference				1.00	0.12	0.12	0.00	0.34	-0.34	0
5. tax abate					1.00	0.77	0.03	0.75	-0.55	0.88
6. chamber						1.00	0.78	0.45	0.22	0.09
7. partners							1.00	0.69	0.65	0.38
8. consultants								1.00	-0.34	0.49
9. loans									1.00	-0.56
10.jobs										1.00

having a conference, which maybe they did not, or had a very minimal investment. The negative relation with having loans may be a fluke, or maybe loan programs did not work. Nothing is exact here, but the coefficients do provide an idea of what is interrelated. Some components are interrelated, as, for example, chamber involvement and having partners; the two may have been part of the same program. In all, it looks as if government and chamber involvement, along with venture capital and tax abatement, are important components to consider in launching an enterprise program.

Correlation data can also be a basis for prediction, a method called *regression analysis.* The results of such an analysis might put you in a position to say that for every $100 invested in the key program components, you could predict the creation of $1,000 in revenue income; funds reflected from tax abatement or government investment were best spent, whereas loans were immaterial. Remember that this is just a hypothetical example, but it does present an example of what research could do here. Although we will not extend the example, correlation or regression analyses could be used to develop a kind of *path analysis* showing interrelated steps for forming an enterprise service center. Arrows in figure 13.3 could be given weights signifying their importance in the paths. We can also calculate the probabilities of whether a correlation or regression statistic could have occurred by chance. Such probabilities could be used to test hypotheses or describe levels of confidence.

Envision how research as illustrated in figure 13.3 could feed into a model for planning new enterprise units, evaluating progress as it grows, and eventually providing a basis for policy decisions. We will also note in chapter 14 how the foregoing can be evaluated in a decision-sciences model.

A Sample Benchmarking Study Using Time-Series Analysis

Importance of a Time Context

Often the sequence or patterns of events—programs, effects, feedback, revision—can have important time elements. For example, the duration of an advertising campaign—deploying advertisements or promotions relative to when they have effects, if any—raises questions about how long certain campaigns will require, or how often they need repeating. We can use a statistical method called *time-series analysis* (example below) to study such patterns. It is more complex than simple one-shot studies, but if you are in a multimillion-dollar development campaign, and the stakes are high, a time-series study may be well worth its costs.

The Benchmarking Approach

Considering the high costs involved and importance of success in promoting adoption of innovations (cf. chapter 9), it is imperative to have a means to measure change. Where are you now? Where do you want to go? How will you know when you get there?

These are known as *benchmark studies.* The best and most objective studies look for hard data, not just opinions or other qualitative observations. Data can be both investment input and performance output as seen across time. For example, has investment in a business incubator (input) resulted in new jobs? Examine figures 13.3 and 13.4 . Both are hypothetical benchmark charts of the above variables. The vertical axis serves both for num-

Figure 13.3
Hypothetical Time-Series Analysis of Effects of Jobs Created. The vertical axis is both investment amount (1 = $100,000) and the number of jobs created (1 = 100). The horizontal axis is time in months. The bottom curve shows investment amount; the top curve shows change in jobs created. In this case, the analysis illustrates small or no effect in jobs created.

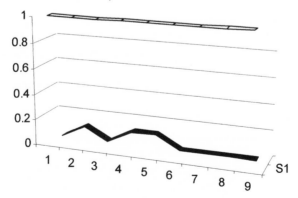

Figure 13.4

Hypothetical Time-Series Analysis of Effects of Jobs Created from Investment in Business Incubator. The bottom curve shows investment amount; the top curve shows change in jobs created (1 = 100). This illustrates the effect of a boost in incubator investment (bottom curve) upon growth in jobs created (top curve). It also illustrates the "lagged" effect across time of job increase coming after incubator investment.

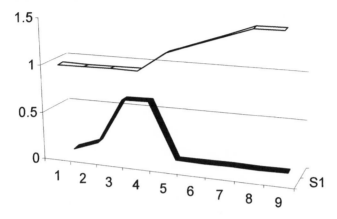

ber of jobs (where 1 = 100) and investment (where 1 = $10,000). The horizontal axis is time in months. Relative to the vertical axis is a top curve benchmarking the number of jobs. The bottom curve benchmarks the amount of investment. In figure 13.4 it appears that although incubator investment varies somewhat, the benchmark curve for job creation is relatively flat, meaning no change in the number of jobs. By contrast, figure 13.5 shows how a momentary boost in incubator investment initiates an upward increase across time of job creation. Note that this benchmarks a "lagged" effect—the boost in investment appears to initiate not just a momentary but an upward increase in job creation. The statistical method of time-series analysis[2] can be applied to test whether this is more than just a chance relationship across time. It will then serve as a benchmark of change—a valuable tool for evaluating investments as well as for planning. Benchmark studies are sophisticated tools for illustrating planning and evaluation for policymakers. After all, shouldn't objective data be used for evaluation where otherwise biased opinions might prevail?

WHO DOES THE STATISTICS?

Obviously, as a busy manager, you will probably not have the time to conduct studies yourself, let alone do the statistical calculations, although the latter can be accomplished easily these days with software for desktop computers. You may want to hire or delegate the hands-on work to a staff member. Or you can opt for a consultant from a commercial research firm or perhaps a nearby university. Your own bottom line in applied research is that there are many powerful new tools available, not difficult to understand, and their applications are easily accomplished by a trained employee or consultant.

CONTRASTS WITH THEORETICAL RESEARCH

Although we have placed the focus in this chapter on improvements in applied research, it is still useful to consider some of the main contrasts with what is often referred to as *theoretical research*. Among the main reasons for examining a bit of these contrasts is that theoretical research—that centered upon discovering or testing underlying principles or explanations—is that research into theory is so highly regarded in university circles that one is apt to devalue applied studies. The point is undertaking what you need to know. For those in search of technological or scientific concepts or principles to commercialize, acquaintance with theory and associated research methods is invaluable. Applied research is not by nature atheoretical; it is often theory put into action. In technology- and science-related businesses, being able to work both sides of the fence—theory and applications—is especially valuable.

If you are not already dealing with research issues or professionals, it can be helpful to sense how goals, attitudes, and institutions may differ in approaches to theoretical and applied research. The theoretical mode is often oriented to concepts within a discipline—for example, physics, sociology, and economics—whereas the applied mode is focused on solving a specific problem. For a contrasting example, one theoretical concept of importance in developmental economics is how innovations are adopted. One can look for answers in several bodies of theory, one of which is the *diffusion of innovations*, where change is seen as a kind of communication process whereby new ideas and reasons for adopting them are spread through society. Another relevant theoretical area is that of the psychology of attitude change, where studies inquire into what is important to us in adopting new attitudes—for example, personal rewards that we seek, or gaining the approval of persons important to us. Theoretical research may involve studies of many different attitudes, types of people, and their motivations. The goals are to come up with generalizations that help in describing, explaining, or predicting adoption or attitude change.

Theoretical research, especially in the academic context, relies upon peer review for quality control. Experts evaluate one another's research findings and proposed contributions to theory. Publications are peer-reviewed. For applications research, quality control is based more upon successful outcomes, social accountability, and acceptance by the practitioner population. The ultimate test is "What works?"

NOTES

1. Perhaps you have heard of or will hear of the so-called Hawthorne Effect. In a study done years ago in a Hawthorne, California, factory, it was found that just receiving some attention, whether or not they were in the actual experimental group, affected the workers' performance.

2. You can read more about time-series analysis in chapter 16 of Frederick Wilson and Peter Monge, *Reasoning with Statistics*, 5th ed. (Fort Worth, Texas: Harcourt College Publishers, 2001).

CHAPTER 14

Decision Science and Risk Analysis

In today's fast-moving business environment, decisions often not only have to be made quickly, but also communicated at the same pace. Moreover, with changing technologies and markets, managers may be making more specific strategic decisions for the first time. Decision strategies of our times are most valuable for meeting these challenges. The theory and science of decision making have not only advanced monumentally in the last several decades, but the fruits of this knowledge have been translated into practical tools for managers and planners. There are clearer premises—that is, logical decision procedures have basic characteristics that, if observed and implemented, will save you money and time plus reduce risk of failures. Some of the procedures are now integrated into relatively easy-to-use software for desktop or laptop machines. In this chapter we present an overview of some of the main characteristics of modern decision procedures. We have also developed several examples or cases to illustrate decision analysis. One is the practical challenge of choosing a server for a small business. Two other cases draw from applied-research examples in chapter 13, namely mixed-media strategies in marketing and the planning and evaluation of an enterprise-services center.

DECISION SCIENCE READY FOR USE

Grounded in results. Sooner or later you must face up to the quality of your decision making. Your decisions have either worked—providing you with advantages in return on investment and the ability to move swiftly to meet competition among fast companies—or your decisions have not worked so well, maybe being costly or even disastrous in some cases. The definition of an effective decision is not found in its elegance or sophistication; it is found in results—what works?

Navigating uncertainty. For many of us—managers, investors, entrepreneurs, government officers—decision making is nothing so new. We have experience and perhaps have had various areas of training in how to make certain types of decisions. Experience ("been there, done that") and intuition ("seems the right thing to do") often serve us well. So why do we need assistance in the form of decision techniques, procedures, or even computer programs? In our practical experience, decision science has improved our decision-making abilities, because it requires

- clear definition of the main or overall goal,
- identification of subgoals that are needed to reach the main goal,
- defining measures, scales, characteristics, or criteria we will use to evaluate our decision alternatives,
- weighting the importance we wish to place on the various measure relative to a decisions,
- defining what we consider to be important risks, negative or positive,[1]
- defining our alternative for reaching the above subgoals and main goal,
- defining or stating the decision situation in a manner understandable to those who could input valuable information, or take results and implement them.

Given the foregoing, decision science and models assist us by providing

- procedures by which associates can provide information or opinions *(preference sets)* regarding the use of the measures in the decision,
- conversion of quantitative measurers into standard scores *(utilities)* that can be examined separately or combined into a multiple score *(multiple utility function)* for a quantitative-based comparison of decision alternatives,
- probabilistic analysis of some set of alternative or measure values occurring as compared with chance occurrence *(Monte Carlo analysis)*,
- various tabular or graphics reports of results,
- methods for analyzing the results for critique, modification, or implementation.

A 10-Step Decision-Analysis Model

Following is a basic 10-step decision-analysis model that, with some exceptions, reflects most approaches to the science. You may think at first glance that this is just common sense. Well, that's basically true, but the admonition is to formalize these steps where possible; have methods for performing them; and do all this in such a way that the approach will be recognized, if not used, by others. You'll see these or similar steps in most approaches described in the endnotes to this chapter. We state the steps in question form:

10-Step Decision-Analysis Model

1. Define overall goal
2. Define subgoals
3. Identify alternatives to be compared
4. Define measures
5. Set measurement levels
6. Quantify preferences
7. Rank alternatives
8. Review and critique results
9. Consider results presentation, communication, and implementation
10. Consider implications for next decisions

SELECTED EXAMPLES

Following are two simplified cases of decision analysis of relevance to entrepreneurs, investors, and officers or executives engaged in economic development. The cases are sufficient to provide an idea of decision-analysis applications without going into technicalities or detail. In-depth and hands-on examples can be found in existing excellent books on this topic.[2]

Case I: Choosing a Server

What's Special about a Server?

Servers are computers that serve as a common resource for company or office files; databases; and management of online service, including e-mail; and may also be the controlling unit for multiple users of printing facilities. The server may also be the repository for files, data, or programs requested online by outside partners of your operation. Servers *time-share*, meaning they can support simultaneous users to an extent. Some small servers look like desktop PCs and some are, although to be of value they typically need more capacity than the usual desktop or laptop machine. Any machine that is set aside for server use is best dedicated to multiple users and not also used as some individual's office PC.

Who Needs a Server?

Chances are that if you are looking for a server, you have access to one already. Maybe it is located outside your office in the computer center of your company, university, or government building. You may be thinking it better to have your own on-site server for such reasons as follows. First, it would be efficient for your staff to have easy access to

- common files of documents, databases, or programs,
- your own internal e-mail or document-transfer system,
- external email and electronic publishing system,
- an ensemble of printers (e.g., for high-speed text, graphics, and special publishing),
- high-security accounting system.

You might also be offering outsider services for clients who log in to your system—for example,

- taking orders,
- making transactions,
- offering files, databases, or electronic publishing,
- offering your outside clients access to e-mail or other online services,
- posting a newsletter for your clients.

Doing the Decision-Analysis Wash

Scenario

Envision that Techaire Inc. is a small firm that mixes chemicals for industrial cleaning companies that contract to do routine space or plant cleanups for technology manufacturing firms where there is a low tolerance for dust and other airborne contaminants. About 80 percent of this $400,000 annual business is done with 12 major customers, the other 20 percent with about 50. Techaire's on-site staff is 15, each using one or two PCs, with 40–60 outside consultants assisting the business and all using PCs and online contact. Keeping more of the company's key information in one machine where it can be supervised, accessed for analyses, and backed up regularly is appealing to Techaire's president, an on-site, hands-on manager who has decided it is time to acquire and implement a server. Staff and consultants will keep their PCs, but the central information of inventory, billing, accounting, and communication will be conducted with a server configuration.

Application of the 10-Step Decision Model

We can summarize the application according to the steps given above:

1. Overall goal: select the best affordable server for Techaire's need

2. Subgoals and measures
   a. Find best affordable price
   b. Operating capacity
      • CPU speed
      • Multiple CPUs
      • Disk size and number
      • RAM size
      • Cache size
      • Communication ports
      • Printer management
      • Internet interface
   c. Quality
      • Scale of 1 (best) to 10 (worst); values given by staff and consultants
   d. Minimize downtime risk
      • Scale of 1 (best) to 10 (worst) for below features; values given by staff and consultants
         • Reliability record
         • Service availability
         • Possible backup server
3. Identify alternatives to be compared
   a. Rambuster is the most expensive ($12,000) and available from a reputable local dealer who offers carry-in service but will come on-site, even at off hours, for a premium price
   b. Compuclone is available from a mail-order firm and, interestingly, has the exact same features as Rambuster but for a much lower price.
4. Gather preference ratings
   a. Staff and consultants gather data and make ratings; data are summarized in a matrix view (table 14.1)
5. Computer manager and president add decision weights
6. Analyze and rank alternatives
7. Review and critique results
8. Consider results presentation and communication
9. Implement results (plan and make purchase)
10. Consider implications for next decisions

Although one person's PC could be configured for certain server purposes, you are far better off having a dedicated machine for this purpose, especially one that is designed and programmed as a server.

Table 14.1
Decision Data Matrix

COMPANIES:	RAMBUSTER	COMPUCLONE	OTHER
Price:	$10,000	$7,500	
CPU speed	2.0 GHZ	1.2 GHZ	
CPUs	two	one	
RAM	256k	256k	
Hard Drive	80GIG	60GIG	
Cache	512k	512k	
Ports	8 com.	6 com.	
Printer cap.	2	2	
Internet	high speed	high speed	
Quality rating	10	10	
Downtime	low	low	
Final ranking	1	2	

Server Basics

A server centrally manages resources that are used by multiple users in a network. It's much more powerful than a desktop PC, and it serves a very different purpose.

Servers are usually dedicated, meaning that they perform no other tasks besides their server tasks. Servers can be used to store files, manage print queues, host the entire company's e-mail, and perform a host of other specialized tasks depending on your needs.

Using a server is advantageous because one person's computer doesn't need to be bogged down by people repeatedly accessing their hard drive. Also, storing the most important data on one server makes regular data backup that much easier.

Case II: Constructing an Enterprise Center

In chapter 11, we presented a brief example of a study involving planning and evaluation of the hypothetical Maintown Enterprise Center (figure 11.1), an organization designed not only for new business planning but for enhancement of existing or relocated firms. In that example, the director of development and her planning team saw three early alternatives for organizing the project:

1. **Fast-track:** This meant getting the project up and running in as short a time as a year. It would bring service online quickly, but at higher initial costs and a lower initial capacity (10 companies being serviced). The main advantage of the fast-track model is that in just about a year the Maintown Economic Development Agency would be up and running some services, at least in an enterprise center, so it could be generating early benefits like attracting new

companies to the area and assisting new ones under development. The main disadvantage of fast-track is that its $1.5 million start-up cost would be inflated somewhat by the physical-plant factor. First, it would have to have to have early access to rental space, including its ready-to-use costs, while building its own structure.

2. **Normal:** This alternative reflected the relatively standard way of doing projects at the time. There would be no demand or provisions for moving up the schedule. The time for project completion is estimated at two years.

3. **Lagged:** In this alternative, if a pause or occasional time-out would have benefits, then the schedule allowed that option. At the outside, including pauses, the center would be completed as soon as three years but not longer than four.

Figure 11.1 in chapter 11 included a fast track for development. You will see some similarity of that earlier figure with the summary decision graphic shown here in table 14.1.

NOTES

1. There is often a common connotation that *risk* refers to a negative happening, as in the risk of losing an investment of time or money or of causing problems. But risk is a probabilistic concept; you may have ways of conceiving of it as a positive alternative—as in hoping that there is little risk of your computer breaking down.

2. For example, see John Schuyler, *Risk and Decision Analysis in Projects*, 2nd ed. (Newton Square, Pa.: Project Management Institute, 2001); Decision Support Software, *Logical Decisions for Windows 95* (Golden, Colo.: Logical Decisions, 1999); Robert T. Clemen and Terence Reilly, *Making Hard Decisions with Decision Tools* (Pacific Grove, Calif.: Brooks/Cole, 2001).

PART IV

Revitalizations

CHAPTER 15

Austin Model: A City Reinvents Itself

If we had time travel so you could visit the Austin, Texas, of the late 1960s, you'd be surprised on several fronts. First, unlike a memory of driving through Amarillo on old Route 66, the path that many Americans who could claim to have visited the state would likely have taken, or one's image of Texas from an old John Wayne movie, Austin would appear as a sparkling, small capital city with plenty of fine trees and parks, and sitting alongside a dammed-up river renamed Town Lake. It is a bit like a southern Madison, Wisconsin, but the weather is better than in that Midwestern state.[1] Enhancing the similarity are their universities and capitol complexes. Like Madison, a sizeable proportion of the population is white-collar, working either in state government, for the university, or in closely associated businesses. But unlike its northern counterpart, Austin has a highly visible minority population, part African American and part Hispanic (virtually all Mexican American), with both groups mostly living in the poorer east side of the north-south central highway (I-3, I-35) rather than the proverbial tracks. Austin is also a mix of western and southern cultures (more south than west)—both the charming and the less so. Charming is the outgoing, friendly manner of people on the street and clerks in the stores ("Y'all come back"). The coveted old-time Driskill Hotel still has colored crystal sugar in cut-glass bowls, sparkling under chandelier lights. But on the overall negative side, still continuing in the late 1960s is the remnant of a racist past, such that a black faculty colleague can't find a barbershop on the campus main street—Guadalupe, or the Drag—that will take him; he must go to east Austin. The UT football team is in its last several years without a black player. Despite their growing population, Austin Mexican Americans are known more to their Anglo counterparts for a few very successful restaurants and mariachi music. There is a raging legal argument over whether children of undocumented parents can be in public schools.

The feel of the American West is found in outlying cattle ranches, including that owned by outgoing president, Lyndon Baines Johnson; Western-wear stores; and the growing popularity of a kind of modernized Western music in occasional Austin performances by popular rocker Buddy Holly, an emerging Stevie Ray Vaughn, and a country boy named Willie Nelson.[2]

Noting the above mention of "creativity," regional economic-development expert Professor Richard Florida of Carnegie Mellon University, in his new book *The Rise of the Creative Class*, designates Austin as the number-two U.S city in this quality, San Francisco being first.[3]

In summer 2002, Austin was still busy plotting a high-tech future. Some 200 entrepreneurs, investors, and planners attended a conference about new directions and opportunities in the electronic-gaming industry.[4]

DEVELOPMENTAL SUCCESS FACTORS

Much as we describe in chapter 6, Austin development is a story validating such success factors as the following:

1. **Vision and partnering:** Key leaders from government, business, the University of Texas, and the Austin chamber recognized that a high-tech economy was an opportune goal in Austin development and had the ability to forge a dynamic partnership to advance toward that goal.

2. **Experience and resources:** Earlier success had its payoffs; this included early establishment of the Tracor Corporation by UT professor Frank McBee, followed by local recruitment of large businesses Texas Instruments, IBM, Motorola, and 3M to locate research-oriented facilities in the area.

3. **University of Texas:** There was ongoing recognition by the University of Texas to cooperate in local and state economic development, including the presence of faculty talent. Included with the University is the IC[2] Institute, which not only participated in developmental activities such as establishing the Austin Technology Incubator, but also researched and documented local development.[5]

4. **MCC recruitment:** There was a highly coordinated effort of the partners to attract the developmental consortium Microelectronics and Computer Technology Corporation to the city.

5. **SEMATECH recruitment:** This landed the chip consortium project.

6. **Spin-offs:** Local scientists and entrepreneurs, though already with large companies, felt motivated to start new businesses commercializing a technology.

7. **Venture capital:** Austin has been a major location for U.S. venture capital and activities to promote investor/entrepreneur cooperation.

8. **The Austin Project:** This was a socioeconomically oriented program to investigate the roots of poverty among Austin's east-side minority groups.

In addition to the aforementioned report from the European Commission Delegation, the Austin development story has been well documented, especially in early research by the IC² Institute's Raymond Smilor and David Gibson.[6]

THE AUSTIN PROJECT

Highly visible among attempts to expand high-tech economic development in Austin was a policy-oriented study and project-development creation designed and implemented by several of Austin's leading citizens—including internationally known UT professors Elspeth and Walter Rostow, among others—with cooperation from Austin businesses, government, schools, the Texas Education Agency, and the IC² Institute. Elspeth, former dean of the LBJ School of Public Affairs, and Walter, a political economist and former advisor to Presidents Kennedy and Johnson, responding to the growing local concern over the economic development discrepancies between the city's east and west sides, developed an initial proposal to study why the mostly minority population of the east side seemed at such a disadvantage in the growing industrial and technological economy.[7] Although labeled *Austin,* the project team developed, tested, and documented the program as a strategy for analysis and application in nearly any city.[8] The strategies of the experiment could be transferred to other communities, and they have been.

The key rationale for the Austin Project was identify and design interventions for breaking what the directors considered a vicious economic-social cycle gripping inner cities, especially African American and Hispanic minorities. Why, in a wealthy and progressive country, and in the face of advances in the social science, should conditions be growing so bad in inner cities? Noted in particular was that current resources invested to break the poverty cycle were so overly concentrated on damage control that attention to prevention was not getting its due. More significant was the charge that even the damage-control efforts were so fragmented and ill coordinated as to be largely ineffective.

For the present chapter, the point is not so much to describe the Austin Project as to concentrate on how the project was able to be organized, planned, and implemented over approximately 15 months. Given initial planning, the essential five components of its strategy can be summarized as follows:

1. Enlist sustained support from local political leaders, including those from the minority groups.

124

New Wealth

2. Aim interventions across life span from prenatal care through educational level to entry of properly trained young men and women into the workforce or professions, keeping a focus also on family life.

3. Gauge and calibrate the level of prevention to match the elevating scale of the problems (unemployment, crime, health, hopelessness).

4. Mobilize aggressively and effectively key social components and institution ("get them on board")—namely businesses, communities, schools, colleges and universities, religious institutions, and relevant social agencies.

5. Especially important: develop steady working partnerships with the Hispanic and African American neighborhoods.

Public announcement of the impending project was on May 6, 1992; following the above-listed five components, a working group of 14 produced a 350-page plan that was released on December 13 of that year. The plan not only launched the project but was the basis of a formal report to the White House Domestic Council under President Clinton on May 4, 1994.

THE AUSTIN MODEL: PREPARATION OF A HIGH-TECH WORKFORCE

The coming of the Microelectronics and Computer Technology (MCC) Corporation to Austin in the mid-1980s signified the city's progress in aiming itself toward the development of a high-tech economy.[9] Accordingly, another key element of the Austin Project was to develop strategies for opening the high-tech workforce to Austin youth. The lead in this component was taken by the University of Texas IC[2] Institute under the title "Austin Model." Activated in June 1989, the overarching goal of the Austin Model was to develop what was called "a global technology transfer infrastructure," with the practical purpose of creating 200 high-tech jobs at a cash cost of approximately $4,200, and to fill 1 million square feet of office space in 10 years. This would be based on commercializing science and technology developed within the University of Texas at Austin; the new consortia, MCC and SEMATECH; and a number of small and large technology-based firms. The financial constraints imposed on the experiment were that no direct funds would be made available for the Austin Model experiment by the federal government, the University of Texas, or the state legislature. All required funds and other resources were to be raised independently through the collaborative efforts among the city of Austin, Travis County, the Greater Austin Chamber of Commerce, and the Austin private sector. The reason for these financial constraints was simply that it would take at least two to three years to raise the required funds from the state legislature or federal government. One could say the leaders were too anxious to start the experiment. The main players are shown in figure 15.1.

Figure 15.1
Austin Model Components.

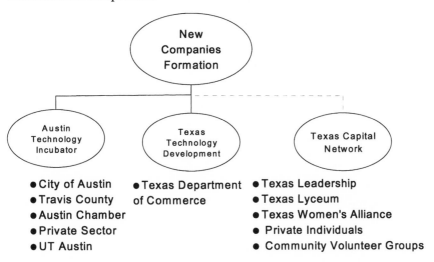

The institute had studied unstructured problems for economic development, technology commercialization, and newer institutional alliances.
It had also performed a number of application research projects. Enough
research was done to develop the key concepts for further experimenta-
tion and evaluation of a technology-transfer infrastructure. Essentially we
recognized that four strategies were important to our efforts:

1. Attract firms to relocate in Austin
2. Retain existing firms
3. Assist existing firms to expand
4. Create entirely new companies, including spin-offs

The key concepts for linking government, business, and academia while
building a robust community infrastructure—talent, technology capital,
and know-how—are shown in figure 15.2.

Successful technology commercialization requires leadership and mechanisms that can link the government, business, and academic sectors. It is
almost imperative at the community level. The community infrastructure
needs to provide talent (entrepreneurs and champions), technology
(ideas), capital, and know-how (management, legal, financial, marketing,
engineering, etc.) linked to market needs. Existing community-based expertise is key to developing and using technology transfer infrastructures.
When these linkages and infrastructures exist, there can be successful technology commercialization.

Figure 15.2
Community Resources.

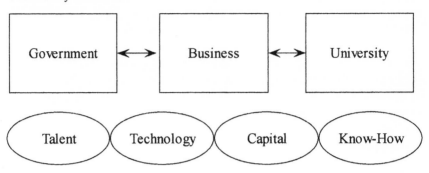

Metrics for successful community economic development by commercializing technology are shown in the following section.

Metrics for Success by Austin Model Stakeholders

A. Government and community
  1. Job creation
  2. Space utilization
  3. Capital creation
  4. Incremental revenues—taxes, services, and so on
B. Private-sector tenants
  1. Capital invested by source
  2. Sales
  3. Time to market
  4. Managerial development
C. Academia
  1. Development of technology entrepreneurship by management curriculum
  2. Successful placement of students
  3. Experimental learning
  4. Royalty and license fees

Manufacturing Technologies Laboratory (MTL)

Among the highlights of the Austin Model was the development of the Manufacturing Technologies Laboratory, a 40-foot trailer housing equipment for computer-assisted design and actual production of plastic-based prototype products created by junior-high-school students. This trailer, which was rotated among selected Austin schools and later locations in the state of Texas and formally evaluated, was developed in association with the National Association of Manufacturing Sciences, including, for Austin, funding by the RJK Foundation associated with the family of George Kozmetsky, former dean of the UT Business School. In early uses, the MTL was moved among schools, offering instant opportunity for hands-on technology education, usually supervised by a volunteer from a manufacturing corporation. Additional MTLs were deployed in other locations in the United States and later commercialized.[10] There was an IC² Institute proposal in the late 1980s to "float" MTLs to Caribbean locations as a seaborne facility traveling from island to island.

AUSTIN 2002

A fast-forward to today reveals, with one major exception, a continuing trajectory of many of the foregoing qualities, fortunately the better ones. Austin is a major Texas city and the center of the nation's largest public university system and endowment. The greatest change by far, however, is that Austin has become one of the world's legendary high-tech economies, and its leaders set out to build it as such. As written by Jonathan Miller of the Trade Section of the European Commission Delegation, Washington, D.C.:

Once known as a sleepy college town of 200,000 residents in 1960 whose principal employers were the University of Texas and the state government, the Austin region has transformed itself into one of the most vibrant high technology regions in the U.S. with a population of almost 1 million. Austin is now a vibrant economy of semiconductor, semiconductor manufacturing equipment, computer manufacturing, and software development, attracting numerous transplants from the likes of Samsung, Motorola, IBM, 3M, and Applied Materials and anchored by the home-grown company of Dell Computer and other software start-ups. Quoting from Fortune Magazine:

For years this green oasis of lakes and hills has served as a geographic and cultural counterpoint to the flatlands, oil money, and cowboy ways of cities like Dallas and Houston. Austin has always been the sort of town where the '60s never really died, where creativity was encouraged and free spirit nurtured.

NOTES

1. Madison and Austin are often compared, both having highly creative universities as well as being state capitals. A personal note from FW: I lived in Madison from 1969 to 1972 as a young faculty member at the University of Wisconsin–Madison. I was eventually attracted to Austin and the University of Texas when the latter was expanding opportunities for young faculty active in research. At the time, the entrepreneurial spirit of Austin was taking root in the expansion of the music industry and birth of an electronics industry. I left to be

founding dean of the Annenberg School for Communication at the University of Southern California in Los Angeles from 1972 to 1985, at which time I returned to UT to occupy the Mary Gibbs Jones Centennial Chair. In that year, the city had put a priority on the development of high-tech industry, influenced very much by the university and business leaders at IBM, Motorola, and Texas Instruments, and encouraged regularly by projects of the IC² Institute and its director, George Kozmetsky, UT Business School dean and cofounder of the Teledyne Corporation, through community service, fund-raising, and developmental research projects, some of which are the core of this book.

2. The legendary late Waylon Jennings, who knew and played with them all at various times, is said to have once remarked to Willie that he was surprised by all the young people and students who came to hear him—not the typical country music crowd, leading him to remark, "Something new is happening to our music." Some have called this the "Austin sound" and attributed it as the beginning of Austin's growth in the music industry.

3. Richard Florida, *The Rise of the Creative Class* (New York: Basic Books, 2002).

4. Home to Origin Systems (eventually acquired by Electronic Arts), Austin has maintained an impressionable foothold in the gaming community for years.

5. Examples of some (but not all) IC² projects are described in William Cooper, Stein Thore, David Gibson, and Fred Phillips, eds., *Impact: How IC² Institute Research Affects Public Policy and Business Practices* (Westport, Conn.: Quorum Books, 1997).

6. For example, see R. Smilor, D. Gibson, and G. Kozmetsky, "Creating and Sustaining the Technopolis: High Technology Development in Austin, Texas," *Journal of Business Venturing* 4 (1988): pp. 49–67.

7. Austin is divided by the north-south Interstate 35, which has been likened to the right or wrong sides of the tracks, an old metaphor especially applicable in southern towns.

8. The best published source of information on this undertaking is W. W. Rostow, "The Austin Project, 1989–1994: Interim Report on Ongoing Innovation," in *Impact: How IC² Institute Research Affects Public Policy and Business Practices*, ed. William Cooper, Stein Thore, David Gibson, and Fred Phillips (Westport, Conn.: Quorum Books, 1997), pp. 63–87.

9. MCC was created in 1982 by leading companies within the electronics industry in response to international initiatives in advanced research that threatened the competitive position of U.S. industry. It was the first high-tech R&D consortium in this country and, over the years, has pioneered research in advanced electronics and information systems, including artificial intelligence and intelligent systems, electronic commerce, electronic packaging technologies, and human interface.

MCC's member companies have included the world's leading computer, semiconductor, and electronics manufacturers, along with users and producers of information technology. MCC shareholders include 3M, Eastman Kodak, General Dynamics, Hewlett-Packard, Lockheed Martin, Motorola, NCR, Nortel Networks, Raytheon, SAIC/Telcordia Technologies (formerly Bellcore), and Texas Instruments.

10. The Amtrol Corporation holds the rights to build and sell MTL models, which now include laboratories for telecommunications and related technologies. The national evaluation was conducted and may be available from Amtrol, the National Association of Manufacturing Sciences, the IC^2 Institute, or Dr. Victoria Williams (williams@icc.utexas.edu).

CHAPTER 16

Project CBIRD: Binational Wealth Creation

The map on the office wall of the *acalde* (mayor) of Matamoreos, Mexico, offers an instant metaphor for binational development. Ranging from Corpus Christi, Texas, at the top to Monterrey, Nuevo Leon, at the bottom, the image strikingly differs from what one sees on typical U.S. printed maps: instead of the usual bland yellow coloring on the Mexican side showing nothing is a detailed map showing complexes of roads, highways, railways, towns, rivers, and a deep-sea port. Obviously, here is a potentially thriving region for binational commerce. And it is. In this chapter, we review the Consortium for Binational Development, known as the CBIRD project for short. Experience from this contributes far more than simply a story of U.S.-Mexico cooperation. It is in many respects a model for binational economic development—or even bicity, bistate, or regional development. The key to success is the ability to create and implement a workable partnership of interest and power sharing; CBIRD is just such a success story.

LA FRONTERIA

The socioeconomic border between the United States and Mexico is not just an international demarcation line along the Rio Grande, or Rio Bravo to Mexicans (see figure 16.1), but a rough, 50-mile thick *La Fronteria* geographic band where, save for the exact legal border marks, there is a veritable bilingual-bicultural region where the nations blend into one another. If enjoying a sumptuous meal on one side or the other of the river, or shopping, because of the blended Anglo-Hispanic culture, you may have

Figure 16.1
U.S.-Mexico Border.

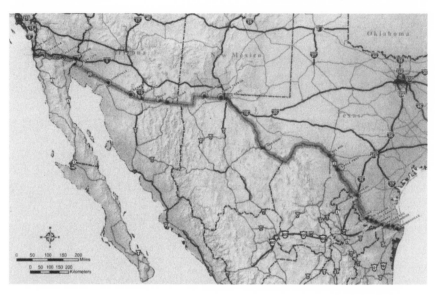

to remind yourself which country you are in. Or, put another way, being in the Fronteria region is also like being in a third, mixed world culture. In business there is much interest in the benefits of science and technology. Except for border-crossing transportation services, businesses, and customs brokers, the small businesses along the border have not benefited as much from NAFTA as their larger counterparts, which may be involved in science and technology commercialization, in inland cities of both countries.

Averaging 25 or so miles both north and south of the river, known as *La Fronteria* to many of its residents, it is a blend of American and Mexican commerce and culture. Most inhabitants representing bilingual-bicultural families travel freely (some daily) in the region and across the legal border for shopping, restaurants, recreation, and work. No matter whether describing the Fronteria or economic relations, NAFTA or immigration, the economies of Mexico and Texas are inextricably tied. Therefore it is quite logical to consider strategies for binational economic development, and that is what CBIRD has been all about.

The Texas-Mexico border region forms a uniquely intertwined, binational, bilingual, and bicultural community. It is a region with its own dynamics, direction, and future. Its population and economy are dynamic and rapidly growing, fueled by NAFTA and their own internally generated short- and long-term initiatives. On the U.S. side, Texas is the second-largest employer in the computer, microelectronics, and telecommunications industries, and does more trade with Mexico than any other state. On the Mexican side, the generalized trade liberalization to all sectors from 1989 to the present has attracted major foreign investments, particularly from the United States, which has increased Mexico's competitiveness in the global economy.

But there are challenges in order to achieve economic growth and sustainable development. The first challenge is how to integrate a binational, bicultural, and bilingual region and its infrastructures into the global knowledge-based economy to maintain its economic competitiveness and maximize prosperity for all of its residents on both sides of the border. The second challenge is how to create jobs, particularly higher-paying technology-based jobs, to reduce the income-per-capita gap between Texas and northern Mexico and the border region. The third challenge is how to empower local communities to develop civic entrepreneurship in the region. The fourth challenge is how to create a culture based on collaboration and cooperation in this binational, bicultural, and bilingual region. The fifth challenge is how to improve rapidly the region's quality of life and protect its environment and scarce natural resources. The sixth challenge is how to build strategic alliances, partnerships, and networks among business and industry, state and local governments, academia, civic organizations, and foundations to address in a coherent and integrated manner the development issues facing the region.

To respond to these challenges and fulfill the vision to create, shape, and build a dynamic and prosperous twenty-first-century Texas-Mexico border region, the Instituto Tecnologico y de Estudios Superiores de Monterrey (ITESM), the University of Texas at Brownsville, the IC^2 Institute at the University of Texas at Austin, and the Houston Advanced Research Center (HARC) established CBIRD as a binational collaborative effort.

CBIRD was officially created on April 7, 1999, when representatives from both sides of the border met at ITESM in Monterrey, Nuevo Leon, to sign the agreement. The partnership not only includes UT-Brownsville, Texas Southmost College, and ITESM, but also the University of Texas at Austin, the IC^2 Institute, and HARC.

CBIRD TODAY

CBIRD is a single institute composed of semi-independent groups and councils, all working together for the common goal of creating a unified border region. Each of these institutions is composed of dedicated organizations and individuals who have volunteered their time, money, hearts, and minds to help shape the future of the region. The groups are organized according to their own self-determined best methods and practices. Each group raises its own membership and determines its own core programs to support the region. CBIRD has a single binational advisory council to help all the groups communicate, cooperate, collaborate, and integrate with each other.

Its goals, as expressed today, include

- assisting in transforming the border-region economy into a knowledge-based economy of technology industries,
- assisting in reducing the real-income-per-capita gap in Texas and the border region and in creating higher-paying jobs,
- identifying opportunities and rethinking, reshaping, and restructuring solutions for the economic wealth and prosperity sharing in the border region,
- assisting the border region in the connections among industry and business clusters and in the building of required partnerships among academic, private, foundation, and government sectors,
- conducting integrated and interdisciplinary joint studies on specific problems facing the border region and generating innovative solutions,
- assisting in the training of the border-region workforce.

The operational components of CBIRD are given below, and their interrelation is shown in figure 16.2.

- **The Binational Advisory Board (BAB),** cochaired by representatives of the University of Texas at Austin, ITESM, and the Mexican states of Nuevo Leon (ITESM) and Tamaulipas (University Valle del Bravo)

Figure 16.2
CBIRD Components.

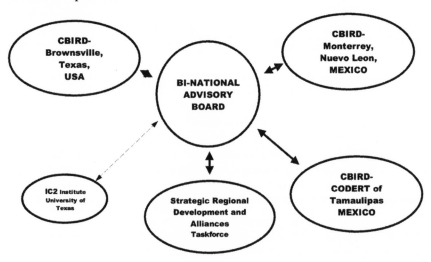

- **Texas Regional Action Council (TRAC),** a committee of founding members of CBIRD from the United States and Mexico

- **CBIRD Institute–Brownsville (UT-Brownsville and Texas Southmost College)**

- **CBIRD Institute–Monterrey (ITESM)**

- **Consejo para el Desarrollo Regional de Transfronterizo (CBIRD-CODERT),** the program at University Valle del Bravo, in Reynosa, Tamaulipas

- **IC² Institute,** providing development of and assistance to CBIRD, and created to respond to these challenges. But, in addition, it was created to establish productive linkages for regional development in this strategic region between the United States and Mexico and a gateway to South America and the world. CBIRD builds strategic alliances, partnerships, and networks among business and industry, government, academia, civic organizations, and foundations to address in a coherent and integrated manner the development issues facing the defined region. It strives to assist the region to forge rapidly its legitimate place in the new economy as a mass-consumption society that is taking shape in the United States and in Mexico.

ORGANIZATION OF CBIRD

Essentially, CBIRD is a binational regional-development initiative with a vision of "one region–one future." Its mission is to promote public-private partnerships in the region in order to transform the economy of the border region into a knowledge-based economy driven by high-technology industry and services. The main goal of CBIRD is to create wealth for, and to share prosperity among, the citizens of the region. In this context, CBIRD's strategy is to play a role somewhat similar to that of the Economic Development Board of Singapore, to attract, retain, and expand U.S., Mexican, and foreign investments in the region.

CBIRD is meant to serve as a catalyst to bring together capital, technology, knowledge, talent, know-how, and networks to create technopoleis or technology-based communities. It is designed to take a proactive binational approach to development to transform the region. It will empower local grassroots communities to shape their own global future in the transformation of the border region into a prosperous twenty-first-century knowledge-based competitive economy. In conjunction with NAFTA, it will assist in building bridges to facilitate greater and integrated binational cooperation and coordination, a prerequisite requirement for the successful transformation and growth of the economy of the region. CBIRD will function as a think tank (and a *do* tank) that is a catalyst to provide a permanent and open forum for academia, the private sector, government (federal, state, and local), foundations, and nongovernment organizations to reshape, rethink, and restructure the economy of the region. In this endeavor CBIRD will rely heavily on the private and government sectors' partnerships as a critical driving force for investments and economic and social change. The partnerships will develop the means and mechanisms to prepare people and places for the twenty-first-century economy, to be globally competitive and innovative, to build capacity and knowledge, and to create high-paying jobs as well as wealth. The partnerships will cover civic entrepreneurship for developing the culture and environment as well as the technology entrepreneurs to attract, retain, and build new firms to generate wealth and prosperity.

CBIRD is an independent, objective, and neutral binational institution. In its management and relations with its partners, it will function as a collaborative and cooperative effort and focus on four main premises:

1. People of the local communities of the region are key
2. Always strive to be the best and deal with the best
3. Always be alert to adapt to a constantly changing environment
4. Leapfrog instead of catching up

The fast-growing population of the CBIRD region is one of its main assets.

As shown in figure 16.2, CBIRD is structured as two institutes: (1) CBIRD-Monterrey, located at ITESM in Monterrey, Nuevo Leon; and (2) CBIRD-Brownsville, located at UT-Brownsville, in Brownsville, Texas. A common Memorandum of Understanding (MOU) coordinates both institutes. An executive director heads each institute.

CBIRD-Monterrey and CBIRD-Brownsville have a joint Binational Advisory Board (BAB), which is composed of a minimum of 8 members and a maximum of 16 members, with an equal number of Mexican and American nationalities. BAB members are selected from the academic, business and industry, government, and foundation sectors. Moreover, each institute can have its own national advisory board formed by members from their respective local communities in order to have a broader representation and wider local input. In their meeting of September 2, 1999, in Monterrey, the founding members agreed to launch the operations of CBIRD for the period 1999–2000 with an interim BAB composed of eight members.

A MODEL FOR BINATIONAL PROJECTS

As said at the outset in this chapter, CBIRD is included here not so much to report on the project but to describe a successful model for a developmental partnership, whether it be among nations, cities, or other entities. It is a most scalable model.

CHAPTER 17

Project Caribe: Prosperity in Paradise

If nations of the Caribbean are to escape their economic marginalization, they need to undertake programs for business diversification and growth, especially where they can take advantage of technologies for the development of new businesses, the invigoration of existing ones, the attraction of new business, and networking. This chapter develops the thesis of Caribbean planning along the lines of the technopolis concept discussed in chapter 8, which offers a vision of economic change based upon partnerships among government, academia, research centers, support groups, existing businesses, and entrepreneurs. The region has considerable developmental potential if the nations could devise and coordinate a regional strategy. The problem, as we see it, is one of leadership. Although cooperating through the so-called CARICOM (the Caribbean Community and Common Market organization), this organization is more known for reconciling trade agreements and keeping statistics. Speaking pointedly, we have observed and heard frequent opinions that CARICOM is also known as a bulky, and not particularly efficient or inspiring, bureaucracy. The nations themselves have developmental ambitions, but mainly ones of diversification beyond tourism.

The technopolis concept facilitates a focus upon how these partnerships—often already to be encouraged—through cooperation and networking can leverage economic development. We are not restricting the concept to an individual nation or city, but the Caribbean basin itself could take upon the characteristics of regional technopolis. The basin needs more vision and leadership to accomplish any grander vision of development. Applications of technology need not mean change at a loss to

Caribbean distinctiveness—namely, its matrix of striking cultures and political heritages—nor to its pristine environments.

But change does mean a broader scope and acceleration in the adoption of innovations, especially an increased focus upon the technologies of modern business, including the workforce, managerial, and entrepreneurial skills to create, grow, and maintain the same. Indeed, attention to the benefits of science and technology may not only facilitate economic growth but also enhance the distinctively Caribbean assets. This chapter reports the results of a five-year project directed toward the analysis of the Caribbean economy and likely directions for growth in an age of science and technology.

Among the conclusions to our work on the island economies is that attention to Caribbean development needs to be accorded to Cuba because economic planning there has included attention to benefits of science and technology even under barriers to technology transfer due to the U.S. trade embargo and the demise of Cuba's economic partnership and technology sharing with the former Soviet Union. Although we include Cuba in the present chapter, we provide a more detailed assessment in chapter 19, which examines the successful commercialization of science and technology within a noncapitalist economic system.

A BIRD'S-EYE VIEW OF THE REGION

Geography of the Caribbean Basin

Typical depictions to the Caribbean focus upon the island nations of the Caribbean basin, a sea south of the United States, east of Mexico and Central America, north of the northern coasts of South America, and west of a chain of islands called the Lesser Antilles. Although the emphasis is usually upon the island nations within this basin, one can also consider the perimeter nations of Central America and northern South America. Further, if the focus expands to include the contiguous Gulf of Mexico, then Mexico and the U.S. states of Texas, Louisiana, Mississippi, Alabama, and especially Florida are within the Caribbean picture. Florida, of course, is an integral part of Caribbean history.

Economic View

Although their economies are often overlooked in descriptions of the Western Hemisphere, when the Caribbean nations are described as a group, they are no small matter. According to data calculated from *The CIA World Factbook* 2001, their aggregate population is 38 million (about two and a half times that of Florida, or the same as Argentina), and their GDP, $139 billion, is a bit smaller than Greece's ($149 billion) but larger than Finland's ($109 billion) and Israel's ($105 billion). Further, if perim-

eter nations of Central and northern South America are included, the collective Caribbean GDP rounds out close to that of Canada ($722 billion).
But the Caribbean island nations are a diverse lot; they differ not only in
geography, backgrounds, and culture, but in population and economic
statistics. Table 17.1 provides a summary.

Among the generalizations drawn from Caribbean demographic and
economic statistics is the dominance of the service sector (average 60.2%)
over industry (23.8%) and agriculture (10.5%). This heavily reflects tourism businesses, but can include offshore banking and similar services.
Most Caribbean nations want economic diversification, which typically
means enlarging the industrial sector by business recruitment, retention,
and enhancement, or by the creation of new businesses.[1]

FROM PAST TO FUTURE

Caribbean nations have a long and rich history mostly overlooked by
outsiders. The edge of their prehistory shows how the islands were first
populated either by chance or trial by native explorers or primitive settlers
boating from the Central and South American mainlands.[2] After their discovery by Columbus in 1492, followed by the colonialization by Europe-

Table 17.1
Caribbean Island Statistics

NATION	Population Census	GDP billions	GDP % Agricul- ture	GDP % Indust.	GDP % Service	GDP per cap.
Antigua & Barbuda	64,006	.52	4	13	84	
Barbados	259,025	2.90	7	17	76	$10,900
Cuba	12,000,000	18.60	7	37	56	1,700
Dominican Republic	8,442,533	43.70	14	31	56	5,400
Grenada	96,217	.36	10	15	75	
Guadeloupe	426,493	3.70	6	9	85	
Guyana	697,286	1.86	35	33	33	
Haiti	6,867,995	9.20	32	20	48	1,200
Jamaica	2,652,689	8.80	7	42	51	3,350
Puerto Rico	3,915,798	38.10	1	45	54	9,800
St. Lucia	152,335	.06	11	32	57	
St. Vincent & the Geradines	119,818	.31	11	18	72	
St. Kitts & Nevis	42,291	.24	6	22	72	
Suriname	427,980	1.44	14	33	53	
Trinidad & Tobago	1,175,523	9.41	2	44	54	8,500
TOTALS	37,339,989	139				

ans, the populations of many islands grew from the importation of slaves.[3] The early economy grew mostly from agriculture.

Today, growth is still from agriculture, with some from mining, but a great deal is from tourism. The *New York Times* News Service (Feb. 2, 2001) reported that there are more than twice as many cruise destinations from the United States in the Caribbean, as in Europe and the Mediterranean.

Yet, despite success with tourism, Caribbean leaders would like to diversify their economy away from the heavy dependence on that one line of business. Not only would further businesses be protection during travel recessions, but they would offer entirely new avenues for development rather than just trying to expand tourism still more. Joking that no giant steel mills are likely to emigrate to the island countries, the question is, what industries and services can be developed? New economic development is emerging (and can be further accelerated) within urban centers where there is a potential for applying the tools of the new economy— that is, applications of information technologies and telecommunications to improve greatly the performance of existing businesses, create new ones, or even attract businesses or partnerships with industries outside the region. These technologies, as in many industrialized countries, form the "smart infrastructure" that underlies much of the new economy. Modernization of the Caribbean is a priority now acknowledged by the regional economic cooperative group CARICOM.[4]

VISIONS OF THE NEW CARIBBEAN

A Bird's-Eye View of the Region

Typical references to the Caribbean, as shown in figure 17.1, focus upon the island nations of the Caribbean basin, a sea south of the United States, east of Mexico and Central America, north of the northern coasts of South America, and west of a chain of islands called the Lesser Antilles. Although the emphasis is usually upon the island nations within this basin, one can also consider the perimeter nations of Central America and northern South America. Further, if the focus expands to include the contiguous Gulf of Mexico, then Mexico and the U.S. states of Texas, Louisiana, Mississippi, Alabama, and especially Florida are within the Caribbean picture. The latter, of course, is an integral part of Caribbean history.

Although often marginalized in descriptions of the Western Hemisphere, the Caribbean nations as a group are no small matter. According to data calculated from *The World Factbook*, their aggregate population is 38 million (about two and a half times that of Florida, or the same as Argentina), and their GDP, $139 billion, is a bit smaller than Greece's ($149 billion) but larger than Finland's ($109 billion) and Israel's ($105 billion). Further, if the perimeter nations of Central and northern South America are included, the collective GDP rounds out to $700 billion, around that of Canada ($722 billion).

Concepts for Interpreting Change

Postindustrialism

The future well-being of Caribbean nations is dependent upon their ability to join, to compete within, and to reap the benefits offered by the changing economy. The models and means for change involve such concepts as the commercialization of science and technology, postindustrialism, and technopolis. The distinction of different sources of economic growth, such as the extraction of wealth from nature (as in fishing, agriculture, and the fabrication of goods), service-industries wealth, and the coming of postindustrialism, by Daniel Bell,[5] as discussed in chapters 1 and 18, all very much apply to the Caribbean economy.

Technopolis Concept

Coupled with the challenges of joining the new economy, especially wealth creation and the sharing of technology and technology commercialization, is the need to conceptualize a socioeconomic model for this development—that is, an overarching concept of the components that can drive or leverage this change. As described in chapter 8, researchers of the IC² Institute have developed such a conceptualization; it is called *technopolis* (plural *technopoleis*) from the combination of the word *technology* and the ancient Greek word for *city*. More concisely: the technopolis is an innovative approach to economic development that involves linking the commercialization of technology with effective public and private initiatives to create new, user-friendly, ecologically compatible infrastructures for economic growth, diversification, and global competitiveness.

Networks and Networking

The ability to forge linkages among Caribbean nations makes theories of networks (as discussed in chapter 6) especially valuable for overcoming the transportation handicaps of an island regional geography. Islands can partner and cooperate so as to form overall networked communities. In many respects, a technopolis is a networked community. Its members often include such components as a university; a ministry or governmental department of economic development; local, state, or national government representation; a business incubator; start-up firms; and investors. Because information and telecommunications technologies support a technopolis, it is quite possible to see how telecommunications investment and operation shrink distances, allowing a given technopolis to "reach out," including how they may form constellations of technopoleis. Thus several Caribbean cities might form a technopolis partnership. A region having multiple technopolis partnerships might itself be developed as a large technopolis—say, the northern Caribbean.

A STORY OF ECONOMIC MODERNIZATION

The potential for economic modernization in the Caribbean takes on the quality of a narrative. Planners have their collective eyes on economic modernization, diversification, and the ability to join the so-called new economy. The narrative has many fast-moving points:

- Success in economic development could trade longtime Caribbean economic marginalization for membership in the burgeoning hemispheric and global economy.

- The quest is not an easy one. It will be necessary to overcome the resisting hands of tradition, entrenched bureaucracies, lack of capital, and the shortage of technology, in both material and human know-how. But there is a desire and a spirit for change.

- The main players in this quest are the four larger island nations—Cuba, Jamaica, Puerto Rico, and the Dominican Republic—known as the Greater Antilles. Haiti is out of the running for now due to a ravaged economy and an unstable political environment.

- Haiti must overcome political and economic instability before modernization is a priority issue. But is it in the interest of other Caribbean nations or any outside the region to assist in the stabilization of Haiti?

- Added to the above are smaller nations—Dominica, St. Kitts and Nevis, Grenada, Barbados, and Trinidad and Tobago—distinguished as the Lesser Antilles.

- Trinidad and Tobago is economically developed due to its petrochemical industry.

- Many nations in the Lesser Antilles are especially challenged for economic development.

- Technopoleis have no boundaries other than the limits of their communication networks. They can reach out for components, collaborate, or combine into larger technopoleis.

- Consider adding to this list of nations the U.S. state of Florida, which as much as any of these players has a Caribbean history and also a role in the economic modernization of the region.

- One can envisage the entire Caribbean group of nations—islands as well as periphery—growing into an all-inclusive network community, a grand technopolis.

- Among cities to examine as emerging or potential technopoleis are Havana, Cuba; Kingston, Jamaica; Port-of-Spain, Trinidad and Tobago; Santo Domingo, Dominican Republic; San Juan, Puerto Rico; and perhaps Miami. Do (or how do) these cities have the makings of technopoleis?

- The technopolis concept can be enlarged to envisage partnerships both within the region and outside of it, just as we recognize that technopoleis are themselves networks of collaboration among government, universities, industry, and other technopoleis throughout the world.

Removing the Distance Barrier

Modern telecommunications cancels the traditional barrier of distance and separation among the Caribbean nations and thus supports technopoleis. The telecommunications infrastructure could also support the linking of Caribbean technopoleis into one regional collaborative technopolis—perhaps of grand dimensions. If a grand technopolis were created, can unification of Caribbean national economies become a virtual economic nation—a power in the hemisphere, a respected player in the global economy? The answer is, "It is possible." But change will only come from great effort or, more so, from cooperation. To examine pathways to change, we examine next individual countries, then consider them as a whole or grand Caribbean economy. But who will lead a grand configuration?

CARIBBEAN NATIONS: A SEA OF DIFFERENCES

A View to the Past

Heterogeneous is a most apt term for describing the human side of the islands. Anthropological research indicates major distinctions among early voyagers from the Latin American coasts. They were not just a single ethnic group or society. The Columbian period brought colonialism, especially with the Spanish, British, French, and Dutch. Africans were brought as slaves and, later, East Indians as indentured servants. In visiting Caribbean island nations one finds a distinct linguistic, cultural, and legal-system flavor stemming from the colonial period. Except for Cuba, which became a communist state after its revolution in the early 1960s, the remaining countries are democracies, mostly following their independence from colonial powers.

Technopolis Candidates

Obviously, the demographics and economic characteristics of a Caribbean nation are an important basis for considering technopolis development. In the following section we provide a glimpse of nations—their most visible characteristics, as well as selected perimeter nations.

Greater Antilles

The Greater Antilles is home to a population of 34 million, or about 70 percent of the total Caribbean island population, including the Lesser Antilles. With the exception of Haiti, definitely not a technopolis prospect, we next examine these island nations in a bit of detail.

Pivotal Role for Cuba

As we said earlier, Cuba is discussed in chapter 19, but for the present discussion we will include a few basic facts. This island nation is the largest in size and population (12 million) of the nations of the Greater Antilles; its 2000 GDP was $19.2 billion. Unfortunately, Cuba receives more attention in the U.S. press for its communist status than for many of its accomplishments, such as a high-quality public education system and universal medical care; services from the latter are sometimes extended in crisis times to other nations, as now with AIDS in Africa. Cuba has also been sufficiently resilient to survive 40 years of economic embargo by the United States. As of this writing, the embargo is slightly lessening, allowing U.S. exports of foods and medical supplies. This is likely to continue for other products and areas. Also, there was the partnership with the Soviet Union, which collapsed during several years of the worst sugar harvests. If it were not for all this, Cuba would probably be a leader in Caribbean business development. Cuba is ready to get the embargo out of the way and get on to new business. If that occurs, Havana has great potential to be a technopolis. It does have a major university and a whole generation of youth whose schooling in math and science makes them well prepared for technology-based business development. This conclusion is affirmed in more detail in chapter 19, where we are able to devote more attention to historical and political contexts.

The Dominican Republic

With a GDP of $44 billion, the Dominican Republic, on the east half of Hispaniola, is the largest player in island economics, except that this reflects the traditional sectors of agriculture, services, and low-wage industry. Economic reform in 1996 has improved the bases for economic growth. High-tech industry development is lacking, but this is a focus of the Instituto Tecnologico in Santo Domingo. Santo Domingo is a technopolis candidate, but it will take a national plan to get there.

Jamaica

Jamaica's economic sectors are almost equally divided between industry and services (mostly associated with tourism), with agriculture a small third. Tourism pervades the beach and forest sections of this island, whereas the business center is in Kingston, a small city with all the urban characteristics of wealth and extreme poverty. There is a priority for new business and technology development, as seen, for example, in the recent deregulation of telecommunications, mostly upon economic premises. Camella Rhone, director general of the Ministry of Industry and Technology, has a vision of tech-based development that is shared by officials of the University of Technology, Jamaica, especially Sandra Glasgow, director of their Entrepreneurial Centre. Having mature industries and institutional support for technology-based economic development puts a focus on Kingston as a potential technopolis.

Puerto Rico

One's first view of San Juan shows how strikingly modern it is—large buildings, freeways, and magnificent resort hotels. Along with these is the outstanding University of Puerto Rico (UPR), which holds its own among any of the U.S. Big Ten universities. Puerto Rico's GDP of $38 billion is large by Caribbean standards, and its economy is among the most dynamic in the region, with the industrial sector as a major component within this. Being largely a bilingual nation, Puerto Rico, or San Juan as a technopolis, can be a meeting place for Caribbean-, Hispanic-, and English-heritage cultures, if not also a gateway to the United States. The latter can sometimes be a bit of a barrier since one will often hear among the islands that Puerto Rico is more like an American state than "one of us." Nevertheless, San Juan is an emerging technopolis, especially with UPR as a resource.

The Lesser Antilles

After the Greater Antilles, the Lesser Antilles is home to about 30 percent of the remainder of Caribbean national populations. They range down from below Puerto Rico to Trinidad and Tobago just off the coast of Venezuela. With the exception of Trinidad and Tobago, the economy of most is based on tourism, especially of a quality of being off the beaten path. Most, however, would desire some diversification of their economy; it is a true challenge to consider strategies for this goal. The networking of small island businesses and perhaps incubators for small and micro businesses is an important researchable topic.

Trinidad and Tobago

This two-island country lies just off the northeast coast of Venezuela. It is distinguished by its prosperity, owing to petroleum and natural-gas processing. The GDP is approximately $9 billion, the largest in the southern Caribbean. Its institutions reflect its strong British heritage. Most of its population of over 1 million lives in Trinidad, and many not far from its major city, Port-of-Spain. The economy is expanding into tourism, and the government has established an economic development corporation

(TIDCO) to promote diversified economic growth. Tobago, as Trinidadi-ans will tell you, remains an example of the early unspoiled Caribbean environment. Trinidad and Tobago offers the quality-of-life dividend for technopolis development.

Barbados

One of the distinguishing features of Barbados is the Grantly Adams International Airport, which is a connection point from larger aircraft to many smaller airlines flying to regional destinations. Though small (population 260,000), this country, once known mainly for sugar cane and rum production, has now developed an industrial sector relative to services and agriculture. Tourism is being promoted. Because of its planned economic diversification and air center, the capital, Bridgetown, could become a point on a southern Caribbean economic network. Our research group found individuals eager and informative in discussions about economic development. Barbados has several cooperative programs with the University of the West Indies.

PERIMETER NATIONS

It cannot be overlooked that the Caribbean economy is interlinked to more or lesser degrees with nations on the perimeter of the region. Because of limits of space, we can discuss these nations only briefly.

Central America

Overview

Although the combined Central American population is only 63 percent of the Caribbean group, their GDP is 84 percent of the Caribbean figure. Most countries of Central America do not have a substantial economic impact upon Caribbean nations. In themselves, Costa Rica stands out for its economic success, Guatemala for its size. All have a linguistic and cultural affinity for the Hispanic-heritage nations of the basin. And there are technological universities located in Panama and Costa Rica.

Costa Rica

This successful country stands out for its political stability and strong economy—an estimated 2000 GDP of $26 billion. The capital city of San Jose is the site of INCAE, an institute for advanced business education. There is also the Universidad de Costa Rica.

Panama

This country is another example of economic success, especially after the downfall of dictator Manuel Noriega in 1989. Its 2000 GDP is estimated at $21 billion. Panama's service industries include banking along with tourism. The city of Panama is host to the Universidad Latinoamerica de Ciencia y Tecnologia.

Guatemala

Just south of Mexico, Guatemala is the largest Central American nation, with a population of 12.5 million and GDP of $48 billion, which reflects a large agricultural component.

Belize

Formerly British Honduras, Belize sits on the eastern side of Guatemala, with which it has had various disputes. Its population is but 250,000, and its GDP is less than $1 billion. However, the location of Belize and the fact that it is English-speaking are assets for future development.

Nicaragua and Honduras

These countries are the poorest in Central America, also suffering from political instability in the 1970s and 1980s. Honduras is another of the Central American countries devastated by Hurricane Mitch in 1999. Its economy is substantially agricultural.

Caribbean/Central America Comparisons

Again, in population, the sum of Central American countries is 63 percent of the Caribbean figure; comparing GDP, Central America is about 84 percent of the Caribbean total. Both regions' GDPs per capita (GDP/C) are similar; all Caribbean island counties have an average GDP/C of $5,835, while Central America has an average GDP/C of $4,660.

Northern South America

The two main countries on the northern coast of South America are Columbia and Venezuela. Guyana, although small and more on the northwest coast, can be mentioned in passing since a relation with Caribbean nations is represented in that the CARICOM administrative offices are located there. Relative to its neighbors, Venezuela and Columbia, and particularly the gigantic Brazil, Guyana is quite small (population about 7,000, GDP $1.86 billion) and has an economy that has fluctuated within the past five years. Guyana has a British heritage.

Columbia

This is a country of political turmoil and recent disputes with America over the drug trade. It has little modernization to offer the economy of the region or association with the island nations.

Venezuela

This country of approximately 23.5 million benefits from petroleum assets. It has offered discounted oil prices to Cuba and several Caribbean countries. Venezuela has a geographic proximity of less than 25 miles at one point from the island of Trinidad. In Caracas, Venezuela offers a graduate center for management education and research, the Instituto de Estudios Superiores de Administracion (ITESA), which has active links with business schools in several U.S. universities. In Barcelona is the University of Central Venezuela, a leader in new economic revitalization research (see chapter 18).

The above countries have a combined population about one and one-third larger than all the Caribbean island nations combined; their combined GDPs are about three times that of the island nations.

Mexico

With a population of over 100,000,000 and a GDP of $865 billion, Mexico is the largest Latin American player in the region. Its inland city Monterrey is an industrial powerhouse and home to the well-regarded Instituto Tecnologico (ITEC).

Border States of the United States

As mentioned earlier, Florida stands out as relevant to analyses of the Caribbean economy. Although northwest of the Caribbean Sea and separated by the Gulf of Mexico, states like Texas, Louisiana, Mississippi, and Alabama can have relevance to Caribbean development. Texas, in particular, has a history of technopolis development. Each has economic-development agencies or departments, and these units do express specialized interests in doing business with Caribbean nations. U.S. chamber of commerce offices are active in the region.

Caribbean Statistics

As we said, Caribbean nations differ not only in geography, backgrounds, and culture, but also in population and economic statistics. Table 17.1 provides a summary: generalizations from these data will be cited as a basis for the economic and technopoleis discussions to come. We will also move to the perimeter of the basin, including Central America, northern South America, and several other locations, including Florida.

Population and GDP Contrasts

Please note the major contrasts in population of these independent nations, which range from 12 million for Cuba down to 42,000 for St. Kitts and Nevis. Similar contrasts are present for domestic production of goods and services (GDP)—in U.S. dollars, or converted to the same, the leaders are the Dominican Republic ($44 billion) and Puerto Rico ($38 billion). Although we have a GDP figure for Cuba, it could be confounded by a difference in calculation for a communist state.

GDP per Capita

Of course, GDP is correlated with population size, so it is illustrative to calculate a GDP/C. The greater this value, the more it indicates a productive economy—that is, more goods and services generated per person. Table 17.1 shows the larger GDP/Cs, omitting that figure for the smaller countries, which are less relevant here. The nations with larger GDP/Cs are Puerto Rico, Trinidad and Tobago, the Dominican Republic, and Jamaica. Note that Haiti is the lowest, which agrees with most economic analyses of this poor country.

Sector Analysis

Going back to GDPs, note how we are able to analyze them in terms of agriculture, industrial, and services sectors. When averaged across countries, as shown in figure 17.1, the service sector is the largest, a usual observation of the Caribbean economy. This mainly reflects tourism but can include offshore banking and similar services. Most Caribbean nations want economic diversification, which typically means enlarging the industrial sector by business recruitment, retention, and enhancement, or creation of new businesses.

Countries with the largest industrial sectors have the greatest potential for technopolis development. Looking back, these are Puerto Rico, Trinidad and Tobago, Cuba, the Dominican Republic, and Jamaica. On the other hand, there are the poorer nations, particularly some of the Lesser Antilles. How can these countries, large and small, richer and poorer, be included in economic-development programs?

Selected Perimeter Nations

As we touched upon earlier, the nations within the Caribbean basin are situated inside a perimeter of nations on all points of the compass. To the northeast are the Bahamas; to the north, the United States; to the east, Mexico; slightly to the southwest, Central America; and to the south, the nations of northern South America. We next briefly examine these nations.

The Bahamas

This British Commonwealth cluster of islands that caters exclusively to tourism and some offshore banking is wealthy. The tourism economy in-

Figure 17.1
Caribbean Economic Sectors.

1. Service 60.2%
2. Industry 23.8%
3. Agriculture 10.5%

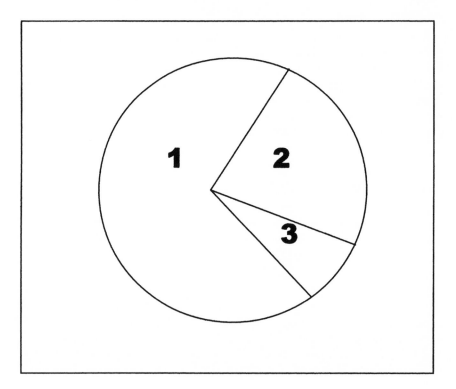

cludes construction of hotels and resorts. The GNP/C is $19,400, larger than any nation of the basin. There is no major evidence we could find of variables supportive of technopolis development, including in the capital, Nassau.

Mexico

The part of Mexico most proximate to the Caribbean nations is the Yucatan peninsula; its cities of Cancun and Cosumel are tourism-oriented. The overall Mexican economy is healthy and has benefited from the North American Free Trade Agreement (NAFTA). The interior city of Monterrey, with its favorable economy and highly regarded Instituto Technologico Monterrey, is a possible technopolis partner. ITEC uses sophisticated telecommunications that improves its attractiveness as a partner; also, there is an affinity with Cuba, Puerto Rico, the Dominican Republic, and northern South America in use of the Spanish language. The historical seaport city of Veracruz is noted for project and conference activities regarding protection of the marine environment.

Central America

Two countries, Costa Rica and Panama, stand out as potential technopoleis sites or potential partners with basin nations. Both have high GDP/Cs for the area. Guatemala, Honduras, and Nicaragua are relatively poor nations with inefficient economies concentrated in the agricultural sector. They are not technopoleis candidates nor partners at this point. The former is mainly agricultural, has problems of political instability, and is currently in disagreement with the United States over drug trade.

A Few Notes on the United States

A Look at Florida

In considering the Caribbean, one can hardly overlook Florida. Although it is a U.S. state rather than a nation, its characteristics are comparable to the Caribbean nations discussed above. Its 2000 estimated population was 15.594 million, about half the total Caribbean figure of 38 million and just slightly larger than Cuba's. Florida's state domestic product for 2000 was approximately $40 billion, somewhat less than a third of the total Caribbean ($144.8 billion). Its sectors, with some combined for comparability with Caribbean sectors, show the Florida economy to be divided among services; manufacturing; combined agriculture, fishing, and forestry; government; trade; finance, insurance, and real estate. The government figure is inflated by Florida's large federal government programs, such as NASA and military expenditures. Services include major entertainment centers in Orlando (e.g., Disney World).

Beyond economics and on the cultural side, Florida is home to similar ethnic groups with cultural heritages found in the Caribbean. Developing a rationale of how Florida and the city of Miami should be considered in technopolis construction in the Caribbean is a genuine challenge.

Texas

Although Texas is a sea away from the Caribbean, it does have major relevance to development. With a GSP of $60 billion, Texas is the 11th largest economy in the world, ranking with or above many nations. Its Department of Economic Development has a Latin American specialty office that includes Caribbean business relations. Further, Texas has four operating technopoleis: Houston, Dallas, Austin, and San Antonio, any one of which is available for discussing relations with Caribbean nations or cities. San Antonio can be seen as a specialist in biotechnology, given the activities of the University of Texas Health Center at San Antonio and its Graduate School of Biomedical Sciences, which have spawned many related enterprises. Houston, long dependent upon the oil economy, has begun to diversify development into petrochemical-related products and services. It also sees itself as a channel for Latin American trade. Rice University, a distinguished private university, prides itself on relations with business and industry. In the Dallas–Fort Worth corridor are a wide variety of telecommunications equipment manufacturers. Dallas, a major banking center, is also home to Southern Methodist University, especially known for its engineering studies. Austin (see chapter 15) is worthy of special mention because it is a widely known example of technopolis creation through partnerships among government, industry, and academia.

On the Potential for Caribbean Technopoleis

Addressing Distinct Values, Priorities, and Needs

In many discussions with Caribbean colleagues, the priority of economic modernization was counterbalanced with the priority of preserving the exceptional qualities of Caribbean life and its environment. The Caribbean's rich ethnic and cultural diversification is to be respected; technopolis planning does not propose social homogenization. Although images of progress include access to new forms of housing, washers, dryers, televisions (and their programs), automobiles, and jobs using machinery or technologies, they can also include the diminution of traditional values, confusions of cultural identity, and an increasing gap between haves and have-nots. The Caribbean's natural environment needs extraordinary respect; the pristine qualities must be protected from exploitation and pollution. ("We don't want to be the next Cancun.") The creation of economic opportunity must avoid engendering social stratification, including among classes and ethnic groups within nations; between rural and urban areas; and between nations, including particular attention to the poorer nations of the Lesser Antilles.

Quality of Life

The Caribbean's culture, values, and environment are an advantage for development; they offer the basis for a rich quality of life, an asset that some technopoleis have lost or overlooked, and can be a powerful drawing card for new businesses.

Technopolis Locations

Technopoleis, although traditionally near or within cities, have not always been spawned by cities themselves. The first great ones in the United States were associated with universities, as with MIT for Route 128 or Stanford University for Silicon Valley. On the other hand, newer or emerging technopoleis in the United States are identified with such cities as Portland, Phoenix, Salt Lake City, or our own Austin. Worldwide, there are emerging technopoleis in cities in Japan, India, England, Russia, and France.

Although there are currently no Caribbean technopoleis as such, there appears to be considerable opportunity for their development, if considered in terms of the components discussed earlier. It follows, therefore, that an examination of Caribbean cities for technopoleis components is a step in the direction of analyzing where Caribbean technopoleis may take root. This is pursued in the remainder of this chapter.

Where Are the Technopolis Potentials?

Criteria Again

Before proceeding, it is appealing to consider several additional features of a Caribbean technopolis. First, although the city may be the likely developmental ground for a technopolis, in the Caribbean island-nation environment, it could well be the center for a national technopolis. So we should not limit our thinking to just cities. Perhaps the Caribbean requires adaptation (or expansion) of the basic technopolis model. Along that line, there is the prospect of expansion through collaboration among Caribbean nations. And, as we have found in no few discussions, why not the Caribbean itself as a mega-technopolis, a network of national technopoleis?

Specific Cities

Before more speculation on expanded technopoleis, we examine selected Caribbean cities as emerging or potential technopoleis. We draw from, and add to, the critical technopolis components listed in this chapter. We do this, however, with the understanding that selected components might not be just within a city, but could be shared (or networked) among several cities or obtained by reaching out to international resources. For example, a technopolis may need training for management or entrepreneurship. It could be delivered via teleconferencing or the Internet from an institution that can offer such services. We can also envisage technopolis networks or even the prospect that a sizeable network itself could become a grand technopolis. We examine the following cities:

- Kingston, Jamaica
- Port-of-Spain, Trinidad and Tobago
- Santo Domingo, Dominican Republic
- San Juan, Puerto Rico
- Havana, Cuba
- Miami, Florida

Including Miami, of course, requires explanation. First, it is a reasonable assumption that the economy and activities of Miami are as much or more intertwined with the Caribbean as any of the above cities. This assumption makes it reasonable to consider the technopolis potential of Miami.

Another decision was to overlook Port-au-Prince, Haiti, because of its current economic, social, and political problems. In retrospect, it would have been interesting to at least gather comparative data on the hemisphere's poorest nation (and its poorest city).

We did mention earlier the challenge of extending developmental activities to the less developed nations of the Lesser Antilles. Whether they could be an adjunct of a technopolis city or within a network is a point to be borne in mind. Following are more thoughts on cities.

Kingston, Jamaica

Technopolis Pros

- Ministry of Commerce and Industry sets priority on high-tech development
- University of Technology, Jamaica, very oriented to technology-based business development; it houses the Technology Innovation Centre
- Jamaica's "Digiport"—telecom and free zone services established near Montego Bay
- Amiable culture
- Recreational environments outside of the city
- Telecommunications deregulation

Technopolis Cons

- Bureaucratic challenges
- Growing urban problems—poverty, crime, congestion, traffic
- Some civil unrest due to economic slowdowns
- Those who want tech-based development may not have a larger image of a technopolis in Jamaican society and culture

Commentary. Located on the southeast coast of Jamaica, Kingston, the capital and commercial center, has a population of just under 1 million.

Among other assets is its location in a large natural harbor, which together with a commercial airport makes it a Caribbean transportation center. Its industrial sector reflects 42 percent of the Jamaican economy. Among its industries (discounting tourism) are light manufacturing, textiles, food processing, rum and beer, paper, and chemical products. Its GDP/C ($3,750) is about midrange among Caribbean nations. The institutions and culture of Jamaica reflect its historical relation with Great Britain, a heritage visible today.

An interview in January 1999 with Camella Rhone, director general of the Ministry of Commerce and Technology, did reveal a recognition that the growth of high-tech industry in Jamaica is welcomed and governmentally encouraged but, as is usually the case, requires entrepreneurship and capital, both of which are limited. Jamaica's population reflects a level of 85 percent literacy, and approximately the same percentage of those 15 and older have attended school.

An important asset for Kingston's business-technology development is the University of Technology, Jamaica. President Rae Davis, an engineer by profession, readily sees technology-based business development as important and possible in Jamaica. This outlook is replicated in the development of the university's Technology Innovation Centre, directed by Sandra Glasgow. Reflecting the business types referred to earlier, the center's rationale statement describes the goal of concentrating developmental efforts in strategic clusters of existing industries.

Kingston surely has potential as an emerging technopolis—an example of initiative to be a player in the new economy.

Port-of-Spain, Trinidad and Tobago

Technopolis Pros

- The Tourism and Industrial Development Company (TIDCO) has been formed to promote economic development
- TIDCO commissioned a large study for economic-development plans
- Officials of TIDCO are knowledgeable and talented
- St. Augustine campus of the University of the West Indies has a business program
- Modern urban services
- Northern coast of Trinidad and all of Tobago island have recreational amenities
- Large petrochemical industry provides national wealth and resources for programs of economic diversification
- TIDCO has opened an industrial park (t-Zone; see chapter 11); seeks high-tech business development
- Technopolis concept is seen attractive, in fact, for both islands of this nation
- Is a major seaport

Technopolis Cons

- High-tech development might move too fast; what technology can be developed in this particular environment and why? What are specific expectations of return on investment? There is no hard data at this point
- Not much on long term expectations
- Not much said about them considering products and services for B2B commerce development
- How does this development fit into social planning?
- Not clear if technological (computers, software, biotechnology) talent is available—how can this be remedied?

Commentary. The population within Port-of-Spain is approximately 75,000; the area from the northwest peninsula through the city and unbroken to Arima is approximately 500,000. Port-of-Spain is the capital of Trinidad and Tobago, the most prosperous of Caribbean nations. It reflects a heritage of British culture and institutions. Its GDP/C in 1999 was $8,500. Its prosperity is due chiefly to the petrochemical industry and the prime location of the harbor of Port-of-Spain as a base for transshipment. Tourism, not a usual major sector of this economy, is growing, boosted by the unspoiled scenery and beaches, including on the largely undeveloped island of Tobago. The Trinidad and Tobago government is undertaking an aggressive program of economic diversification. One consequence of this is the establishment of TIDCO.

Technology-based business development is definitely on their agenda, as seen in the recent establishment of their Technology and Innovation Park on the grounds of a former air-force base. Descriptions of the park include invitations for technology-based businesses. Its mandate includes a business-incubator operation. There is a specific business interest in software development. As for technopolis development, beyond an obvious focus on Port-of-Spain, TIDCO vice president Andre-Vincent Henry added, "Why not all of Trinidad and Tobago?" After all, there is a concentration of technopolis components—existing businesses, an industrial park, entrepreneurs, an educated workforce, and very attractive living environments in rural Trinidad and Tobago. There is the St. Augustine campus of the University of the West Indies. Port-of-Spain is equipped to be underway as an emerging technopolis. And there is the time factor—perhaps now is opportune.

Santo Domingo, Dominican Republic

Technopolis Pros

- Instituto Tecnologico de Santo Domingo (INTEC) is an excellent resource for higher education, management training, and economics research

- The telecommunications industry is rapidly developing modern services
- Santo Domingo is urbane—that is, hotels, restaurants, entertainment, banks, transportation, and so on
- Beneficially located in northern Caribbean Sea, south of north Atlantic—to Haiti (other side of island), Puerto Rico, Cuba
- Large economy ($43.7 billion), which can be used to support economic diversification
- Opportunities in biotechnology research for agricultural sector
- Given economic reforms and aggressive economic progress, time is right for technopolis visioning

Technopolis Cons

- Variation in economic sectors—which sectors offer the most promising return on investment?
- Subject to hurricanes
- No technopolis-type visioning seen in government or university reports, or from interviews and conversations. No visible program for small-business development, incubators, and so on
- Some corruption
- Street crime
- Untrained labor force
- Some inefficiencies and problems with banking services
- Challenge to electric power capacity growth
- Central regulatory system for business sometimes arbitrary

It seems to us that the Dominican Republic is less visible to U.S. business than are other major Caribbean countries—probably the Americans' fault, but the Dominican Republic could promote itself more in world business, especially if it could offer competitive advantages in the high-tech areas (perhaps offshore manufacturing, offering B2B services, and the like).

Commentary. Santo Domingo, the capital of Dominican Republic, is rich in history, as it was the base for Spanish explorers and conquerors in the New World. It is positioned as an excellent seaport. Santo Domingo is among the larger cities of the Caribbean. Although sugar growing is a major part of the Republic's economy, industry (e.g., sugar processing, textiles, mining, and tobacco) accounts for 31 percent of the 1999 GDP of $43.7 million, which is large by Caribbean standards. Its GDP/C is $5,400.

Santo Domingo is a prime example of where considerations of technology-based economic change can be concentrated in a university—in this case, INTEC. In personal meetings with Professor Alpolinar Veloz, chairman of the Economics Department, we learned of his department's ongoing study of trends in the Dominican Republic's economy, including their interest in technology-relevant sectors. Since 1996, the economy of the Dominican Republic has been the focus of a program of reform, which has now contributed to visible investment and growth. The services and agricultural sectors, as would be expected, are labor-intensive, thus distracting from technology investment. This is exacerbated by the illegal influx of low-wage Haitian workers.

INTEC hosts the CAMPE (Centro a Apoyo a la Micro, Pequena y Mediana Empresa) program. It is a USAID project aimed at assistance to micro-, small-, and medium-sized enterprises. This program is an excellent example of introducing training for modern management methods and services, including business incubation.

In conclusion, it is clear that as opportunity presents itself, Santo Domingo, with the assistance of an institution like INTEC, can build technopolis qualities. INTEC also supports REDINTEC (*red* is "network" in Spanish); Internet access to the university's departments, faculty, and programs; and an e-mail service. It is as modern as you will find in any U.S. university.

San Juan, Puerto Rico

Technopolis Pros

- Modern, very strong economy
- Large and sophisticated University of Puerto Rico
- Obviously a Caribbean link and gateway to the United States
- Educated workforce
- Entrepreneurial talent; exchange with United States in same
- Base for U.S.-Caribbean exchange, including Spanish- and English-speaking cultures

Technology Cons

- No (or unknown to us) ministry or agency for high-tech economic development

Commentary. San Juan is a twenty-first-century city in all respects. The University of Puerto Rico ranks alongside any of the U.S. Big Ten universities, if not higher in some comparisons. Technopolis development is there if San Juan wants it.

From the vantage point of other Caribbean countries, however, San Juan and Puerto Rico are seen as distinctively American. "Puerto Rico is just another U.S. state," you will hear. For good or for bad, this is the attitude, and it will have to be taken into account in any technopolis-development program that involves cooperation with other Caribbean cities.

Havana, Cuba

Because we have devoted chapter 19 to Cuba, we make only a few summary points here.

Technopolis Pros

- A public school system internationally recognized for its excellence, especially in mathematics and the sciences; this has great potential for technology-workforce training (although Havana does not have sufficient jobs for them)

- A public health-care system lauded for offering access to all; teams from this system sometimes provide emergency services in other countries

- The University of Havana is large and sophisticated, an excellent resource for national or urban planning; as noted during our visit in 1999, there are budget shortages which was learned especially in discussions about computer equipment and services

- Discounted oil-import agreement with Venezuela

- Some emergence of software-development capabilities; Cubanet is among the best Caribbean and Latin American Web sites

- Development of their first industrial park (related to us by a ministry official)

- President Castro and the Society of Cuban Economists have been supporters of the major World Economy and Change conferences in Havana, January 1999 and 2000

- Cuba has been capable of meeting overwhelming economic challenges—namely, the 40-year U.S. embargo, the loss of their economic partnership with the former Soviet Union, and several devastating losses of their sugar crops

- The U.S. embargo will surely come down within the next several years and is now relaxed in areas like health care and agricultural products

Technopolis Cons

- Cuba's economy has been strangled for 40 years by the U.S. embargo, which has included blocking loans from regional and international banks; accordingly, because of basic development needs, a technopolis vision has not been able to emerge

- Not sure how technopolis visions, especially capitalistic, could fit within marxist priorities—how does high-technology business development square with the confrontations posed by *Das Kapital* or *The Communist Manifesto?*

Commentary. Havana is the premier among Spanish colonial cities of the Caribbean. Although appearing in disrepair, the colonial charm is unfettered from inroads of tacky modernization—fast-food restaurants, strip malls, and the like. It is a city of some million inhabitants (the country has 12 million) just 90 miles south of Key West, Florida (Key West is closer to Havana than to Miami). As noted in chapter 19, the estimated GDP of Cuba is $18.6 billion. GDP/C is markedly low (1999 estimate $1,700); however, this may be a distortion caused by calculations of this figure in communist economics. With very little exception, as a collectivist economic system, the Cuban government owns and controls all commerce ("Think of Cuba as one large corporation," you may hear from officials) and therefore garners all wealth generated by that commerce. In a quick look, those assets are directed back into government direct expenses—operations, defense, business subventions, other subsidies, costs of operating the nation's universal education and health-care system—and then, as an operation of a Communist economy, the remaining wealth is "distributed to the people."

Currently, Cuba's greatest asset is its "human capital," a young and educated workforce. Its talent for economic survival, if not growth under adverse conditions, could give it advantages for new urban development for a technological age. As for the abandonment of the U.S. embargo bringing abrupt change, this might not be the case, as it is said that President Castro wants to jointly administer the change so as to avoid unmanageable consequences, as in the fall of the Berlin wall.

To improve one's understanding of contemporary Cuba, and to see through the veil of outsider propaganda, it is important to read directly some of the writings and documented speeches of President Castro. In the 1990s, he concentrated on the negative impacts of the neoliberal (free-market) economic forces driven by the G8 nations upon the smaller nations of the world, including his own. As in marxist philosophy, Dr. Castro argues that the bourgeois nations are creating and maintaining their wealth at the expense of the proletarian nations. Strictly from an economic standpoint, communism, despite condemnation for its restrictions upon travel, free speech, and democratic rights, is a form of socioeconomic change, and hence deserves close study. It underlays the founding of the former Soviet Union and served Mao Zedong in raising millions of desperately poor and uneducated Chinese out of the rice paddies. We are not advocating it, only the study of it, including within the largest country in the Caribbean.

With its large population and GDP, Cuba (and its capital, Havana) could be the largest island-nation player in the development of Caribbean technopoleis.

Miami, Florida

Technopolis Pros

- A large and robust economy
- Has a special organization (the Beacon Council) formed to promote economic development
- Very close links, culturally and economically, with Latin America and the Caribbean
- Gateway to Latin America
- Bridge between English- and Spanish-speaking societies
- Transportation hub of the Caribbean
- For last several years has wanted to develop high-tech industries

- Miami technopolis would fit well within, and add value to, a Caribbean technopolis network

Technopolis Cons

- Not much evidence or expression about technopolis-type vision, including from its developmental group, the Beacon Council; In their Web site, the council declares that they do not want to be an "experimental" city (a technopolis is not meant as an experiment)
- Community of Cuban expatriates is dedicated to Castro's downfall, making pro-Cuba programs difficult to undertake

Commentary. Miami (and greater Miami) is a very large urban area on the southeast coast of Florida. The 1999 population of Miami was 2,166,800, or almost the population of the country of Jamaica (2,652,689). It is a trade and transportation center for Latin America and the Caribbean. It has long considered itself "The Gateway to Latin America." In the last five years it has taken an interest in encouraging high-tech business development, but does not see itself developing along the lines of a Silicon Valley, Austin, Texas, or Boston Route 128 model. The city has formed the Beacon Council to promote and communicate about economic development. Reports from the council are regularly updated and linked to the Miami Web site, which can be found with any search engine.

Conceptualizing Miami as a Caribbean technopolis can arouse feelings among Caribbean thinkers about U.S. hegemony. Given Miami's size and economic clout, would it not tip the balance among Caribbean partners? Of course, there is a similar question about Florida itself.

POTENTIALS FOR ECONOMIC CHANGE

Technology Commercialization

We have already referred to the new economy as using technology to change the way we do business and the businesses that we do. Spelling this out a bit more includes (1) developing technology as a business in itself, (2) developing a new business based on technology commercialization, (3) using technology to improve an existing way of doing business, and (4) designing an entirely new way of doing business. Following is a true example.

1. An entomologist scientist-consultant discovers that a female insect's egg cycle varies with the density of the contiguous population. He believes this phenomenon could be a basis for measuring grain infestation that could replace the burdensome task of cutting into a storage sack and drawing a sample handful of grain to then be visually examined for infestation. As research is his business, he sells rights to the use of his invention for product development and goes on to do more R&D.

2. The entrepreneur who bought the rights proceeds to develop a tool for easy sampling (much less than a handful) and automatic egg testing. Manufacturing and selling this tool is a successful new business based upon technology commercialization.

3. A grain-shipping company licenses use of the tool in order to offer it as part of its contract for improved shipping services.

4. A silo-design business group licenses the tool's detection technology in order to incorporate it into its next generation of grain-storage models—a new way of conducting the business.

Technology in the Caribbean

Although the Caribbean is acknowledged to house its share of so-called developing countries, it is not without certain technologies and a desire for more. Of first importance are those directly relevant to existing businesses. This can also be said for technologies used in social services.

Some business applications (or desires for the same) include

- biotechnology in agriculture and aquaculture
- new equipment for extractive industries, as in mining
- improved technology for building construction
- refining product production in petrochemicals
- marketing and transactions, as in resort and vacation marketing
- banking
- entertainment industry
- Internet and computer-application service providers (ASPs)
- hotel and resort plant management
- food processing and packaging
- fish processing
- light manufacturing
- distilleries and bottling
- seaport and airport management
- teleports
- applications in electronic commerce

ELECTRONIC COMMERCE

The coalescence of computing and telecommunication has made possible new intelligent networks that serve key components of business. One is network-based wholesale and retail marketing, now typically called *business-to-consumer* (B2C) commerce, where goods and services are sold or ordered over the network, now typically the Internet. The other is *busi-*

ness-to-business (B2B) networking, whereby components of a business or businesses themselves can interact.

BUSINESS-TO-CONSUMER

In a Caribbean Marketplace

Envision a Caribbean Internet super-site that offers all of the colors, sounds, movements, and almost the smells of a Caribbean marketplace. Customers carry their shopping baskets to stores offering fruits, organic foods, art, clothing, and sample snippets of music that a credit-card entry allows them to transfer the entire recording of to their home computer. The market is global. A British shopper may simultaneously be examining goods with electronic visitors from Japan, Italy, and France; a rancher from the tiny sun-bleached town of Globe, Arizona; or a furrier in the snow-bound city of Oulu, Finland. Visitors to the Caribbean art exhibit can exchange opinions in the exhibit's chat room, including with a "critic of the month." Already on the Internet are Caribbean recreational sites offering virtual tours and booking services to potential vacationers.

Skip the Middleman

Caribbean products, traditionally limited to sales through distant middlemen, can now directly reach a worldwide market, thus keeping more profit at home, including profits for their own banks and e-commerce technology providers. Moreover, we can envision a network of small vendors offering their goods and making sales transactions through the use of a grand Caribbean e-commerce Web site. Technologically, small e-commerce businesses can be established and grown with only a modest investment—namely, a personal computer, Web-design software, and a reliable and reasonable-cost Internet services provider (ISP). Of course, there are also the business model and managerial requirements. What does the business entrepreneur have to sell? Who will buy it? How reliable are product supplies? What are the costs of operating the business (space, utilities, employees)? What is the source of start-up capital? What is the probable return on investment? All these are typical questions to be answered in a business plan. Incidentally, most small e-commerce businesses, like other small businesses, fail for lack of marketing capability, often an overlooked factor on a business plan because of the lack of experience in this area.

New wealth generation from Caribbean e-commerce can come from the ability of many micro and small businesses to conduct businesses on their individual Web sites. Like ease and cost of access for any of a nation's Internet users, the technology and an Internet universal-service policy should facilitate small-business incubation and growth.

Small firms require substantial help in starting and growing. A national or regional program for assisting in micro- and small-business development for e-commerce is a necessity. National or local technology-business incubator programs have demonstrated success.

The Big Picture of B2C Growth

From 1997 to 2000, the economic sector of e-commerce in the United States grew from $600 million to $3 billion. In the fourth quarter of 2000, the U.S. census estimated that retailers rang up $5.8 billion in online sales. Leading into 2001, the annual rate of growth is now estimated at 120 percent. During the Christmas gift season of 2000, estimates were that 8 to 10 percent of all gift expenditures were done online.

However, the season brought with it a new twist: growth of online business from traditional brick-and-mortar purveyors' sites begin to gain on sales from sites of originally established dot-com companies. Thus, book buyers may have gone to the sites of Barnes and Noble or other traditional booksellers rather than to Amazon.com. Shoppers looking for small goods, inexpensive cameras, clothing, or toys may have gone to discount store Target's site rather than to specialty online sites. Target and others offered wide-ranging post-Christmas online clearance sales.

Like examples of Wal-Mart moving into a U.S. rural market and wiping out most small would-be competitors, we may see this economic pattern in the growth of consumer e-commerce. Mega-retailers offering large varieties of goods, low prices, efficient transactions, and shipping may suck up small online companies, forcing them to become suppliers to them if they are to remain in business. This has many implications for existing or would-be Caribbean online retailers. They will have to offer unique products (as in the marketplace example) not found from the online giants, and, further, make their products attractive for large-retailer inventory and be able to meet the challenging demands of supplying a huge company.

Lessons from Failure

During the 1999 Christmas season in the United States, at least 39 percent of online shoppers experienced delivery problems. Not only were customers disappointed, but the problems led to a visible drop in company stock value. It was all a rude shock to the burgeoning e-commerce businesses. A major lesson from this failure was that success in this method of doing business was more than a pretty Web site. It was the ability to deliver promptly and accurately on orders. Problems analyzed and mostly corrected by Christmas 2000 from this failure in order-filling operations were

- insufficient stock
- inadequate communication with suppliers
- inefficient packaging procedures, supplies, and packers
- poor transportation capacity
- insufficient workforce
- inability to track orders from receipt to fulfillment
- lack of interactive communication with customers

Home Products

Our research has noted Caribbean "home" products—for example, fruits, herbs, organically grown foods, cigars, seafoods, crafts, and art— that are prime for e-marketing. This is not to overlook vending Caribbean music for direct purchase and downloading from the Web—now a reality. Also recognized are early uses of Internet-based marketing and transactions by Caribbean resorts and realtors.

Caribbean Tax Advantages

Just as countries like Bermuda have traditionally attracted businesses by offering tax advantages, dot-com companies have looked for similar opportunities there and elsewhere in the Caribbean. Although a topic of current debate, the tax interpretations are that the sale takes place at the site of the server, and therefore tax, if any, comes under the regulations of the host country. Shipping of merchandise may come from another country—for example, mink from Canada or Norway. This creates a great opportunity for Caribbean countries to incubate dot-com sites, if not for a local company, then as a service for outsiders—similar to the business of becoming an application service provider (ASP). The longtime telecommunications provider Cable and Wireless has upgraded facilities for Internet traffic, and so have new competitors who have been able to enter the business due to deregulation. A new firm called HavenCo, operating from a sea platform, plans to grow its services up to 5,000 servers. E-commerce-oriented banks are necessary, and they are developing as with the Bank of Bermuda and the Bank of N. T. Butterfield and Son.

Citizenship, as with the United States, may be the tie-in for tax liability. However, as with one Vince Cate, who renounced his U.S. citizenship for one from Mozambique (for $5,000 over the Internet), tax liability may be changed.

Clearly the foregoing tax advantages are a case where technology is ahead of regulation and offers opportunity for new business ventures and policymaking in the Caribbean.

Serving CARICOM Protocol III

CARICOM's Protocol III calls for Caribbean entry into new areas of business. It is noteworthy that e-commerce networks would directly serve this new industrial policy (see chapter 6) to develop a market-led economy that uses new technologies so as to be competitive in world markets. Not to be overlooked are the business opportunities a regional e-commerce developmental program could bring to less-developed countries of the Lesser Antilles. A challenge to CARICOM is to promote micro- or small-business e-commerce incubation in these nations.

THE B2B REVOLUTION

Metacapitalism

As attractive as the new market opportunities of consumer-oriented e-commerce are, the revolution having the most economic impact is likely from the networks that allow large businesses to form communities of B2B networks.

Evolution of Outsourcing

The evolution in mass manufacturing systems during the last century brought with it not just the production line but the practice of outsourcing. Traditionally, a vertically integrated company manufactured most of the components of its products, then assembled them for market. Eventually these companies—for example, automobile and home appliance firms—found it increasingly cost-beneficial to have others manufacture these components, such as electrical, drive-train, and suspension parts for automobiles, or small electric motors and valves for washing machines and refrigerators. This practice has come to be called *outsourcing*.

As management of outsourcing has been greatly assisted by the development of modern telecommunications, companies and their outsourcers have themselves become a large virtual organization of the business. And one can add to this network the marketing components—research, promotion, sales, and follow-up. This phenomenon is further enhanced as we have seen outsourcing grow far beyond just submanufacturing operation; it has expanded to encompass service firms that provide advertising, communications, human resources, comptrolling, legal assistance, and scheduling services.

The Coase Theory of Transaction Costs

"Transaction cost" is a significant consideration in decisions about outsourcing. What are the costs of locating the best outsourcer, negotiating an agreement, and then figuring the time and expense of setting up and

carrying out the agreement? These factors, according to Coase, affected the development of outsourcing. Now, with the costs of transaction falling exponentially with telecommunications advancements, especially with the Internet, the outsourcer relation is more quickly and effectively established. This is among the driving variables of the new economy and of tremendous significance to Caribbean economic development. It is also an underlying variable in the technopolis concept—the networking of the critical components of economic development.

What are the Caribbean business opportunities as outsourcers? Is it in the delivery of goods from light manufacturing (e.g., clothing and textiles), agricultural products, music, aquaculture, marketing, and advertising services for the region, or especially tailored computing and telecommunication services? Who are the potential partner companies for B2B operations?

Network-Based Communities

Networks of B2B commerce can only exist on the platform provided by sophisticated telecommunications. Outsourcer manufacturers and service providers can stay closely linked with their business customers' needs. Obviously many of the B2B services themselves can be delivered over a telecommunications network. Taken in a large view, B2B networks can be characterized as communities. The more services available via the network, the more value. These network-based communities are a fundamental component in emerging technopoleis.

Growth of Core Firms

Perhaps the most significant change driver of B2B networks is that they can support a basic redesign in business organization. As we examine network factors, note how they can fit Caribbean applications. As firms have been able to outsource increasingly their manufacturing and service needs, less is needed at headquarters or at the core firm. This means less space, less production equipment, fewer personnel, and the potential for less required capital. Significant capital and risk shift to the outsourcer.

The core company owns the business (its brand), manages its network, and concentrates on the fundamentals of return on investment. Modern companies like Dell Computer and Cisco Systems fit this model. Since both of these companies create their products by order and specification from buyers, one can consider the customers as more than an abstract market. They become an identified population, another component of the company's network community. It supports a "pull" system of commerce where products are created to meet user specifications—a natural for a network. To help visualize this model, think of the businesses of being a contractor or consultant. What do they own? Usually not equipment, inventory, or a large payrolled workforce. Contractors or consultants own their reputation, their image, and their ability to compete for project bids and generate a profit if they get the job. A core business is the center of the action—of the networked community—planning and managing, raising capital, designing and marketing products, taking custom orders, outsourcing manufacturing, handling funds, and hopefully posting profits.

What are the core-business opportunities for the Caribbean? Very visible have been large vacation and resort businesses, but the question needs be raised whether a business has its core located (site, employees, financial center) within the economy of a Caribbean state where growth contributes to national economic development rather than to profits for an outside owner. What are new core opportunities? They may lie within e-commerce development, as subsequently discussed.

1. Core-business characteristics
   - Ownership of basic concept for commercialization
   - Highly sophisticated marketing research
   - Entrepreneurial, investment, and managerial talent
   - Superior telecommunications network and information technologies assistance; a "smart" building
   - Cooperation with government
   - Capability to develop outsourcer network or join or create a larger networked community

2. Outsourcer business considerations
   - Fundamental B2B capabilities
   - Manufacturing or services to offer
   - Capital availability
   - Plant development
   - Possible industrial-park involvement
   - Telecommunications and computer services
   - Transportation infrastructure
   - Utility (power, water, sewerage) capability
   - Environmental impact
   - Workforce availability
   - Technical workforce training

3. Importance of the "smart" infrastructure
   To drive home a key point: note the array of knowledge and information requirements inherent in the foregoing considerations and the importance of a smart infrastructure to support them. The requirements of the core business are related more to knowledge and information than to space, plants, and workforce. Outsourcer businesses, while needing knowledge and information, also have their physical requirements. Cities or countries wishing to invest in industrial parks should give thought to how physical requirements for businesses change in the B2B era.

4. Situating businesses

A core business development may do better in a downtown entrepreneurial environment close to government, banks, marketing firms, investor groups, and perhaps a university. Outsourcer businesses fit the industrial-park concept. But both need the telecommunications (smart) infrastructure. Mismatches may bias a city's development efforts toward creating sunset rather than sunrise industries.

SOCIAL SERVICES

The smart infrastructure can also support new social services such as telemedicine; distance education; and telecommuting, where work can be brought to the employee rather than vice versa, thus saving on traffic and fuel costs. Distribution of these social services, as well as their costs, can be shared among villages, towns, cities, and even nations. The infrastructure opens up opportunities for collaboration with perimeter nations, including the United States. It brings new opportunities to the smaller islands of the Lesser Antilles.

E-Commerce Business Opportunities

Given the economic analysis and observed country priorities, especially desires for development, and existing, planned, or desired businesses, we surmise that the following areas of commercial development are significant to include when considering the coming of the new economy and e-commerce to the Caribbean. They include support of e-commerce services as well as marketing. For example:

- Computer sales and services
- Software development
- Computing ASP businesses
- ISPs
- B2B telecommunications services
- B2C electronic commerce; "kits" for start-ups
- Management of shipping and transshipping services
- International banking
- Improvements in oil, gas, and mining businesses' management networks
- Real estate development, construction, and sales
- Commercial programs for workforce training
- Development of commercially operated business incubators
- Offshore fabrication services

Examining technology-based business creation, including e-commerce, is one view of change in the Caribbean.

THE CARIBBEAN AS A VIRTUAL ECONOMIC NATION

Creation of Technopolis Networks

How are technopolis networks formed? Mainly they grow out of entity-to-entity links, then the multiplication of links among numerous entities. A network community grows as each potential member has something to gain from joining it. Caribbean technopolis networks have not typically been—but they could be—a result of a program of an overarching organization such as the Organization of American States, the World or Inter-American Banks, the United Nations, or CARICOM.

One can visualize technopolis networks as self-creating much in the way the Internet has expanded. An organization—perhaps the component of a technopolis—can join the network, then it is up to them to decide whom their regular contacts will be or which networks they join or create. The Internet example is opportune since technopolis networks now depend upon the Internet. The organization could be a new business, industrial park, or business incubator undertaking development; a mature business seeking new lines of development; an R&D corporation; a university or technological institute; a government unit; or any of the components of the technopolis presented in chapter 8. What do other members of the network, resource centers, new partners, resources, or portals to larger networks have to offer this new member of the network community?

CARIBBEAN TECHNOPOLIS NETWORKS

Reflecting the foregoing discussion, very important in this chapter is that when we refer to technopolis construction in the Caribbean, it need not be restricted to an individual city. It can refer to businesses within cities, but also how components can join much larger regional or international networks. The city is the pole or base point out from which can develop the links.

In review, among emerging Caribbean technopoleis or base points are cities like Kingston, Jamaica; Havana, Cuba; Port-of-Spain, Trinidad and Tobago; Santo Domingo, Dominican Republic; and San Juan, Puerto Rico. On the Caribbean perimeter are Miami, Florida; Caracas, Venezuela; Panama, Panama; and San Jose, Costa Rica. Technopoleis can reach out internationally. We could conceive of networks forming such as Kingston–Palo Alto–Boston–Austin–Caracas. Or a networked technopolis component might be built not only among businesses or cities but also among technological universities in Kingston and Santo Domingo or Florida International University in Miami. Typically, however, we refer at first to cities because that is where the businesses (poles) are located, or the component universities or other components of the technopolis wheel.

VISIONS OF CARIBBEAN TECHNOPOLEIS

Given the concept of learning-and-innovation poles, the nature of knowledge and information in the new economy, and the telecommunications network capability, nothing geographically limits the scope, or footprint, of a Caribbean technopolis—a very significant quality for island nations traditionally constrained in growth by their island geography. There is potential for a powerful technopolis network—a step toward economic competitiveness in the hemisphere (membership in NAFTA?), competitiveness in the global economy, and the end of the economic marginalization of the Caribbean.

In the Caribbean, technopolis coalitions—networked communities—could develop around nations of the

- Northern Caribbean,
- Southern Caribbean,
- Hispanic and Spanish-speaking Caribbean.

Or it might develop around nations with economic specialties in

- biotechnology,
- overall technology commercialization,
- computer application-service providing,
- software development and commercialization.

A most ambitious vision is the entire Caribbean as one vast technopolis, which leads to a further vision—namely, a virtual economic nation.

TOWARD A VIRTUAL ECONOMIC NATION

When we consider the potential character of the Caribbean as a virtual economic nation, we have the option of including all basin island nations and the perimeter nations of Central America and northern South America. And there is Florida, and surely Miami, to keep in mind.

Population

The total population of the combined Caribbean, Central America, and northern South America region is 132 million, a little less than the populations of France and Germany combined (150 million) or roughly half the population of the United States (276 million).

Gross Domestic Product

Collectively, the nations of the Caribbean can make sense as an economic entity. The island nations have a combined GDP of $139 billion. For some international comparisons, the island-nation Caribbean GDP is only a bit smaller than that of Greece ($149 billion) and Portugal ($151) but larger than that of Finland ($109 billion) and Israel ($105 billion). With an eye toward the closest U.S. state, the Caribbean GDP is three times the size of Florida's ($40 billion).

If we considered a Caribbean technopolis as including Central America and northern South America, the combined GDP is $700 billion—around that of Canada.

Gross Domestic Product per Capita

On the less impressive side are the averaged GDP/Cs in the region (tables 17.2 and 17.3). The average island Caribbean GDP/C is $5,879; Central America's is $4,660, and northern South America's is $5,567. Compare these with the nearby Bahamas ($19,400), or Florida ($33,900), Greece ($13,900), Portugal ($15,300), and Israel ($20,300).

Although the size of the Caribbean economy can rank with the sample countries listed above, again, their GDP/C is not impressive, which we can interpret as meaning that they have visibly less economic productivity. Accordingly, they are challenged to streamline their economies lest they continue to be uncompetitive with other nations. Moreover, failure to compete in the new economy will exacerbate this marginalization.

COMPONENTS FOR A REGIONAL TECHNOPOLIS

Examination of economic data for Caribbean cities, especially seen as a group, readily suggests the importance of visioning the entire Caribbean as an economy, with technopolis cities as development nuclei or poles. Note how the network reveals a consortium structure among major cities of the region—indeed, a mega-technopolis.

Within the Caribbean, consider the collective technopolis-oriented characteristics; they compare with many countries of the world. We can see the option of including Florida, which, although politically distinct in the area, does share economic, cultural, and linguistic affinities.

Nine Major Cities

- Caracas
- Havana
- Kingston
- Miami
- Panama
- Port-of-Spain
- San Jose

- San Juan
- Santo Domingo

Seven Major Institutions of Higher Education

- University of the West Indies
- Universidad de la Habana
- University of Puerto Rico
- Florida International University
- Institute for Advanced Studies in Administration, Caracas
- University of Technology, Jamaica
- Instituto Tecnologico de Santo Domingo

CARICOM

If we talk of regional cooperation among Caribbean nations, CARICOM must be examined.

Background

The Caribbean does have a near-term history of national cooperation dating back to the establishment of the British West Indies Federation in 1958. By 1962 this was replaced by an organizational evolution leading to the formation of the Caribbean Community and Common Market (CARICOM), which came into effect in 1973 by the Treaty of Chaguaramas, of which establishment of a common market was the aim (slogan: "One market, one economy").

CARICOM Today

Currently CARICOM has 16 member nations, with Cuba and Haiti as observer nations. The secretariat is located in Georgetown, Guyana, where administrative functions are maintained. Meetings of the Community Council of Ministers rotate among countries.

CARICOM's Three Objectives

1. Economic cooperation through the Caribbean Common Market
2. Coordination of foreign policy among the independent member states
3. Common services and cooperation in functional matters such as health, education, culture, communication, and industrial relations

In passing, it should be noted that CARICOM maintains an excellent public communications program through available project documents, minutes of meetings, and administrative reports. The CARICOM Web site is first-rate, making the information about the organization easily available.[6] The information-sharing operations of CARICOM are an excellent example of communications within a networked community.

Protocol III Industrial Policy

In 1998, CARICOM member nations agreed to an industrial policy as an amendment to its original treaty. Its 27 articles begin with a preamble expressing their determination to promote and establish a sustainable balance between industrial development and environmental integrity.

The goals and actions of Protocol III are to have the distinct qualities of an orientation toward modern development and cooperation among nations. It is in many ways the type of network we have been discussing; our approaches are complementary.

For illustration, we provide selected excerpts from articles most relevant to our discussion at hand:

Excerpted from Article III (Objectives of the Community Industrial Policy):

- "A market-led internationally competitive and sustainable production of goods . . . "
- "Public and private sector collaboration . . . "
- " . . . balanced development . . . bearing in mind the special needs of disadvantaged countries . . . "

Excerpted from Article IV (essentially about the implementation of Article III):

- " . . . coordination of national industrial policies of Member States."
- "[The] establishment and maintenance of an investment-friendly environment . . . "
- "[The] organization and development of product and factor markets."
- [The] development of required institutional, legal, technical, financial, administrative and other support for the establishment or development of micro and small economic enterprises throughout the Community."
- [The Council for Trade and Economic Development] shall collaborate with competent organs and bodies of the Community and the private sector, establish criteria for according special consideration to particular industries and sectors . . . . Such criteria shall include, in particular, arrangements relating to the prospects of the industry for successful production integration."

Excerpted from Article V:

- "The Community shall adopt appropriate policy measures to encourage the development of competitive micro and small economic enterprises in Member States."
- "[promote the] development of the capacities of national and regional agencies for micro and small economic enterprises, including the creation and entrepreneurial centres, by organizing technical assistance inclusive of planning, delivery and evaluation of support services to the sector."[7]

TOWARD ECONOMIC COLLABORATION AND POWER

At this point we would hope the reader shares our judgment that Caribbean nations, including those on the perimeter, have excellent prospects for joining the new economy. But cooperation and collaboration loom as large challenges. A complete Caribbean technopolis can never be attained without economic and political partnership among its nations.

This is not a new challenge to the peoples of the Caribbean. It existed on the edge of Caribbean prehistory. For five millennia before the arrival of Christopher Columbus in 1492 the Caribbean archipelago was a mosaic of different languages, cultures, and economic strategies. Early Europeans misunderstood this diversity as a simple distinction between "Caribs" and "Arawaks." In fact there were many distinct groups who sometimes competed, sometimes cooperated, but always had to take into serious account both the cultural and political complexity of the islands and the constant involvement of people from outside the Caribbean. All of these characteristics of the region still hold today.

ACKNOWLEDGMENTS

A rich resource as well as source of great pleasure were those individuals from the Caribbean who took time to answer our (FW and VW) Project Caribe questions, suggest better ones, and provide us with cultural and political insights. Truly, the Caribbean is not only among the most beautiful environments of our earth, but its citizens are blessed with a sense of culture and outreach. We have made many new friends. Among them:

Adams, Claudio U. CAMPE, University of Technology, Jamaica
Brijmohan, Manjula. Institute for Private Enterprise Development, Georgetown, Guyana
Comas Pulles, Raimundo. Presidente, Sociedad Cubana de Logistica, Cuidad Habana, Cuba
Davis, Rae. President, University of Technology, Jamaica
de Gannes, Debbie Lewis. American Chamber of Commerce, Port-of-Spain, Trinidad and Tobago
Figuras, Miguel. Scientist, Ministerio Para La Inversion Extranjera y la Colaboracion Economica, and Ministry of Tourism, Ciudad Hababa, Cuba
Fundora, Roberto Morfa. Presidente, Asocion Nacional de Economistas de Cuba, Cuidad Habana
Garcia, Ibrahim Ferradez. Ministry of Tourism and former Minister for Foreign Investment and Economic Cooperation, Cuba
Glasgow, Sandra A. C. University of Technology, Jamaica
Gomez, Gustavo R. Machin. Cuban Interests Section, Washington, D.C.
Hamel, Maria de la Luz., Ministero del Comercio Exterior, Republica de Cuba, Cuidad Habana, Cuba
Henry, Andre-Vincent. TIDCO, Port-of-Spain, Trinidad and Tobago
Hitchie, Jim. Cuban Investment Corp, Vancouver, B.C., Canada
Isa, Umaru Yerima. Embassy of Nigera, Cuidad Habana, Cuba
Marrett, Christine. Distance Education Centre, University of the West Indies, Kingston, Jamaica

Miller, Errald W. Cable and Wireless, Jamaica
Rhone, Camella. Director General, Ministry of Commerce and Technology, Jamaica
Rivera, Victor M. President's Office, University of Puerto
Seeberan, Marjorie. University of the West Indies, Mona Campus
Stockhausen, Becky. American Chamber of Commerce, Jamaica
Vargas, Silvia Hernandez. Ministeripo de Educaion Superior, Cuidad Habana, Cuba
Veloz, Apolinar. Professor, Instituto Tecnologico de Santo Domingo, Dominican Republic
Walker, Patrick B. Deputy Programme Manager, Caribbean Community, George-town, Guyana

Finally, for their sponsorship of valuable programs, we also thank the Societies of Cuba and Latin American Economists, who, with the support of President Fidel Castro, organized the two excellent international conferences in Havana on economic development in the region.

In closing, to all of our new Caribbean friends, may our paths cross soon again.

Fred and Victoria

NOTES

Materials for this chapter were drawn from the book manuscript *Technopolis Construction in the Caribbean: Coming of the New Economy* by Victoria Williams (available at http://www.ic2.org/Victoria%20Williams-presentation.pdf). The research was undertaken under the IC[2] Institute's Project Caribe, directed by Frederick Williams.

1. Diversification is a frequent topic in Caribbean economic-planning discussions and publications, as, for example, a conference of telecommunications business leaders conducted in March 1998 in West Palm Beach, Florida, sponsored by Northern Telecom; the author (FW) spoke on the social benefits of telecommunications.

2. Samuel Wilson, ed., *The Indigenous People of the Caribbean* (Miami: Florida Anthropological Association, 1998).

3. Ron Ramdin, *Arising from Bondage: A History of the Indo-Caribbean People* (New York: New York University Press, 2000).

4. CARICOM supports a sophisticated Web site—see http://www.caricom.org/.

5. Daniel Bell, *The Coming of Post-Industrial Society* (New York: Basic Books, 1976).

6. http://www.caricom.org/.

7. *Protocol III, INDUSTRIAL POLICY;* the provisions of the Protocol replace the Articles on Chapter Six of the Caribbean Common Market (CARICOM) Annex (except Articles 43, 48, and 49) to the Treaty establishing the Caribbean Community, Georgetown, Guyana, 1998.

Treaty establishing the Caribbean Community and Common Market signed at

Chaguaramas on 4 July 1973; revised Treaty of Chaguaramas establishing the Caribbean Community including the Caricom Single Market Economy, Caribbean Community (CARICOM) Secretariat, 2001.

Protocol III, Industrial Policy (Protocol Amending the Treaty Establishing the Caribbean Community)

http://www.carisom.org/archives/protocolIII.htm

CHAPTER 18

Anzoátegui: A Venezuelan State of Change

Oil wealth is as much of a challenge as gift, and it could even be a curse. Upwards of one-third of Venezuela's $146.2 billion GDP is in the petroleum sector, as is 80 percent of the value of its exports. These, of course, fluctuate synchronously with the world oil price as it is buffeted by OPEC decisions, political pressures, or outright war. A petroleum economy driven by these external factors, as well as internal dissension over distribution of assets, often draws important attention away from and leaves neglected a nation's other economic sectors and potentials. Realizing this dangerous path, the current Venezuelan leadership is entertaining an aggressive program of cross-investment, meaning investment of as much oil wealth as possible in the development of economic diversification, including strategies where science and technology are seen as a source of replenishable wealth. As described throughout this book, such major change involves dynamic and newly creative business and development thinking, enterprise strategies, cooperation of government with universities, foundations, and perhaps the addition of catalytic components such as enterprise-development centers or technology incubators. Fascinating in the new Venezuelan economic-revitalization strategy is the intended development, including with science and technologies of agriculture and aquaculture, of a vast virgin region of gleaming seacoast; lagoons; and green, fertile hills in their state of Anzoátegui ("an-swa-tee"), named for an Indian hero in the country's struggle for independence from colonial Spain. The Anzoátegui story as reported in this chapter is unfolding this very day as a classic of institutional cooperation, the tried and true, "think globally, act locally," and the valued philosophical underpinning of this book: aiming for measurable enhancements in the quality of everyday life.

The most important issue in this chapter is whether the sophistication and likely impact of the Anzoátegui developmental initiative could carry over to stimulating—and perhaps leading—needed regional development of the Caribbean basin. As said in chapter 17 and the book *Technopolis Construction in the Caribbean: Coming of the New Economy* by Victoria Williams,[1] the Caribbean basin is ripe for new economic development and diversification, but to date no island nation has taken the initiative to try for much beyond its own borders. Could success on the national level give Venezuelan leadership a role in Caribbean regional development with an Anzoátegui technopolis as its hub? We return to this question to conclude this chapter.

NORTH AND SOUTH AMERICA: MAYBE TIME FOR A NEW RELATIONSHIP

Of course, development does not take place in isolation. Venezuela is strategically located at the wealthy midpoint—in talented and energetic people, economics, natural resources, and scenic beauty—between North and South America. What of the North-South connection, and, in particular, the connection with the United States? Be cautious of stereotypes; much is changing.

As I (FW) was reminded—and as many longtime citizens of the Venezuelan capital city, Caracas, may tell you—a warm turn in North-South relations was marked on a day in 1961 when a young, attractive American president, John Fitzgerald Kennedy, knelt and placed a ceremonial wreath of flowers in their historic Panteon, at the tomb of Simon Bolivar, leader of the revolution that freed Venezuela and South America from colonial Spain. President Kennedy was traveling in support of his *Alianza para Progreso* (Alliance for Progress), the first major U.S. initiative for economic cooperation after years of inattention and looking away from dictators since lobbying South America to the Allied side in World War II. Regretfully, the young president was gunned down the next year, and not much else of a policy nature emerged for another three decades, until NAFTA was under discussion.

Thinking back, I could not help but be awed by the historic change I have seen in my life as an American about things Hispanic. When I was a young grade school student in the Chicago of the 1940s, electing to study Spanish as a school elective was an exotic choice to my parents. My father, whose sports were swimming and shell racing, allowed me to enroll in Spanish so long as I would sign on and keep up with the school swimming team. (*Comencé a aprender español. Valioso a este día.*) Now, looking back, there has been a very significant change in things Hispanic in our country.

America, through waves of immigration from Spanish-speaking countries—especially Mexico, but also Puerto Rico, Central America, the Caribbean, and some of South America—has enlarged its Hispanic qualities in language, culture, and international interests. Spanish is by far the most popular choice for second-language study in U.S. schools. And for a culinary touch, there was the report several years ago of how salsa was beginning to outsell ketchup in this country. We are a far less Anglocentric country than four decades ago when President Kennedy launched his *Alianza;* now we are better prepared for North-South, Anglo-Hispanic partnerships.

A FEW NOTES ON VENEZUELA

The northern perimeter countries of South America became of interest to us in the course of IC² Project Caribe (see chapter 17) research because, as we have said in the preceding chapter, if you include the economies of Caribbean perimeter countries with those of the island nations, the combined GDP exceeds that of Canada. Venezuela stands out among the perimeter countries because of its burgeoning petroleum-driven economy and, as we are currently learning, its sophisticated initiatives for economic diversification. Table 18.1 summarizes key statistics of the country.

Geographically, Venezuela is about twice the size of California, its population of 25 million a little less than twice Florida's.

Economically, the Venezuelan GDP ($146 billion) is around 80 percent of that of the much larger—in land and population—Brazil ($176.5 billion). Venezuela's GDP has been in a decline, and this is one of the causes of public hostility to current president Hugo Chavez. On the other hand, we include Venezuela in this book because there is a sophisticated campaign for economic revitalization, diversification, and development of the Anzoátegui state, with its land-rich Unare region. Details are described in the next sections.

Unare Basin–Anzoátegui Study

Among the studies of Group Tech/SUDIL is an examination of the economic-development potential of the Unare river basin in the northeastern state of Anzoátegui entitled *Development Sustentable and Diversificación of the Economy of the Unare Basin and its Economic Connections with the Metropolitan Zones of Anzoátegui State and the Caribbean.* Unare North was selected for a number of reasons, including the economic potential of the region, the similarity of its municipalities, and opportunities for technology-enhanced agriculture and aquaculture as well as other potential sectors, including light manufacturing. No less important were the peoples of the region—their capabilities, specializations, and motivation for economic development.

Table 18.1
Venezuelan Statistics

DEMOGRAPHY

Population estimate	**23,916,810**
Infant mortality	**25.37/1,000**
Life expectancy	**73.31 years**
Literacy	**91.10%**

ECONOMY

GDP (2000 estimate)	**$146.2 billion**
GDP per capita	**$6,200**
Labor Force	**9.9 million**
in agriculture	13%
in industry	23%
in services	64%

LAND USE (1993)

Arable	**4%**
Permanent crops	**1%**
Pastures	**20%**
Forests	**34%**
Other	**41%**

Among the goals of this study are design of a technology-based incubator for new businesses, namely *Proyecto de Centros de Innovación e Incubadoras de Empresa*. It is this project, in particular, that led to an exchange of visits between scholars of Project Anzoátegui and the IC² Institute of the University of Texas at Austin, which operates the world-renowned Austin Technology Incubator described in chapter 11.

Creation of Tech/SUDIL

Tech/SUDIL is a conglomerate—interdisciplinary, interuniversity, and international—organized for academic as well as practical study of the potential for the development of proposed concepts and new technologies for the transformation of economic and social (life quality in services and opportunities) environment of the region. A fundamental objective is to achieve these goals in joint participation with the local governments and communities, so as to set in motion sustainable, technology-assisted development. Organizations comprising Tech/SUDIL and selected individual scholars, managers, and other key persons are listed in an addendum to this chapter.

Much as described in earlier chapters of this book, as well as in other examples of revitalizations (see part IV), cooperation and partnerships are key to success in developmental projects. To achieve these objectives requires an integration of conceptual points of view as well as cooperation in the implementation of proposals and technologies. Such cooperation is agreed upon at the outset through *covenants*[2] among the universities as well as with the local governments, private businesses, and consulting firms.

Achievements in the First Six Years

Among the actions and results of the Tech/SUDIL during the first six years of its existence are

- establishment of covenants between the rector of the University Brandemburguesa of Cottbus and the rector of the Central University of Venezuela for the creation of an interuniversity, interdisciplinary research group (June 9, 1997)

- selection of the community *urban-metropolitana* of the High Mirandinos for study of integral development

- selection of the rural-Andean community of the High Basin of the River Motatán, and the creation of the organization ECOPÁRAMO

- agreement among the deans of the faculties of the Departments of Humanities, Education, Architecture, and Engineering, for the conformation of the Group in the UCV and the faculties of the departments of Medicine and Agronomy (June, 1997)

- covenant between the rector of the University of Göttingen and the principal of the Central University of Venezuela to be incorporated to the project (July 1998)

- covenant between the rector of the University of the Andes and the rector of the Central University of Venezuela to be incorporated to the project (July 1998)

- start of the conversations with the Universities of Potsdam (Germany) and Complutense (Spain) for the execution of an International Course of Management of the Local Development (September 1998).

- Constitution of support for the project, through the Project of Investigation: "Analysis of the University Capacity to Generate Technologies Adequate and Adapted to the Needs of the Local Productivity," which itself is carried out under the coordination of Dr. Miguel Breceño, in four universities—UCV, USR, ULA, and UDO (July 1998)

- presentation of the Viable Project of Technologies to the Sustentabilidad and to the Development Integrated Localities for the firm of covenants with the following institutions: Venezuelan Institute of Planning (IVEPLAN), Program CIARA, PROA (Program Axis Orinoco–Hurry), Business of Software Specialized CALIBRUM, Viceminsterio of Development Regional Cordiplan, National Institute of Investigations Agrícolas (INIA) (March to December 2001)

- approval of financing on the part of CONICIT for the start of the Project for the Development Integrated of Communities of the Axis Orinoco–Hurry (July 2001)
- participation in the First Journeys carried out in Zarazas, which counted on the participation of the local authorities and the community (September 2001)
- participation as *conferencista* in the First Forum Venezuelan-German of Science and Technology, with a *ponencia* upon the Venezuelan Initiatives for the Technological Innovation, by means of Centers Temáticos (October 19, 2001)
- *pasantía* in Germany with the fundamental objective to bring up to date the knowledge upon development and *sustentabilidad* and to prepare the program of the job of the scientific shop of exchange among German and Venezuelan professors it carried out in Port the Cross (October 2001)
- execution of the second step of interdisciplinary study for the Development Integrated Localities of the Basin of the River Unare with the participation of 40 Venezuelan and German professors (November 2001)

The View Ahead: Venezuelan Leadership in Regional Economic Development

As introduced early in this chapter, the success of this project raises the challenging question of whether Venezuela should take more of a leadership role in Caribbean regional development where we have found an absence of regional leadership (see chapter 17). An Anzoátegui technopolis could be the center and driver of a greater Caribbean Basin economic sphere, as well as a vital hub for entire Southern Hemispheric development. Note the network of close contact among regional Caribbean technopolis cities, coupled with longer range, occasional ties with major North and South American centers.

ADDENDUM: TECH/SUDIL ORGANIZATIONS AND INDIVIDUALS

ORGANIZATIONS

Of. 5–1—Postal Section 47342, Caracas, Venezuela; tel/fax: [58] (212) 919-8070; e-mail: mibricen@reacciun.ve

Participating: University Oriente (Venezuela); University G. M. Ayacucho (Venezuela); University of the Andes (Venezuela); University Simón Rodríguez (Venezuela); University of Texas at Austin (United States); University of Cottbus (Germany); University of Göttingen (Germany)

INDIVIDUALS

Professors of the Central University of Venezuela (Professor, Área of Especialización)

Miguel Angel Briceño Gil, Coordinador of the Project
Karenia Cordova, Geografía, Energy and Environment
Luis Gamboa Cuencas Hidrográficas, Cartografía
Antonieta Camacho, Historia of Venezuela
Marine Light Barreto, Filosofía Moral
July Cubas, Geografía and Environment
Euclides Sánchez, Psicología Social of Communities
Karen Cronick, Psicología Social of Communities
Fernando Giuliani, Psicología Social of Communities
Ainoa Larrauri, Idiomas Modern
Gustavo Hernández, Comunicación Social
Elvira Sergent, Educación
Belkis Marcano, Educación
José Luis Rodríguez, CENAMB
Pains González, CENAMB
María Isabel Peña, Faculty of Architecture and Urbanismo
Adriana González, Faculty of Architecture and Urbanismo
Rebeca Sánchez, Faculty of Engineering (Sanitary)
Maritza Rivas, Faculty of Engineering (Geodesia)
Naime Wagdi, Faculty of Engineering (Vialidad)
Yuri Medina, Faculty of Engineering (Hydraulic)
Henry Blanco, Faculty of Engineering (Sanitary)
José García, Faculty of Sciences (Chemical)
Gonzalo Boggio, Faculty of Veterinaria (Maracay)
Raúl Hernández, Faculty of Veterinaria (Maracay)
Adriana Florentino, Faculty of Agronomy (Maracay)
Brunilde Mendoza, Faculty of Agronomy (Maracay)
Lia Tovar, Escuela of Public Health (Medicine)

Participating Professors of Other Universities

Hildamar of Rengifo, University Simón Rodríguez, Coordinadora Tech/SUDIL USR
Nancy Álvarez, University of the Andes, Tecnología Educational and Coordinadora Tech/SUDIL ULA
Nory Pereira, Colls University of the Andes, Centro of Investigations of the Dwelling
Elisabeth Torres, University of the Andes, Instituto of Statistics and Computation
Priscila Guevara, University of Oriente, Coordinadora Tech/SUDIL UDO
Rubén Aparicio, University of Oriente, Instituto of Oceanografía
Jeremy Mendoza, University of Oriente, Instituto of Oceanografía
César Lodeiros, University of Oriente, Instituto of Oceanografía

Miguel Guevara, University of Oriente, Instituto of Oceanografía
César Graciani, University of Oriente, Departamento Biology
Oscar Samer, University of Oriente, INDESA (Barcelona)
Fidelina Moncada, University of Oriente, Workshop of Formation of Investigators
Fights Ortega, University of Oriente, Workshop of Formation of Investigators
María Milady, Rodríguez, University of Oriente, Workshop of Formation of Investigators
Glory Bejarano, University of Oriente, Workshop of Formation of Investigators
Joust Rodríguez, University of Oriente, Workshop of Formation of Investigators
Lourdes Reyes, University of Oriente, Workshop of Formation of Investigators
Yaneis Obando, University of Oriente, Workshop of Formation of Investigators
Raisa Yanez, University of Oriente, Workshop of Formation of Investigators
Rafael Alemán, University of Oriente, Workshop of Formation of Investigators
Edith Salazar of Marcano, University of Oriente, Workshop of Formation of Investigators
José Francisco Rodríguez, University of Oriente, Workshop of Formation of Investigators
Zulay Poggi, University Great Mariscal of Ayacucho (Barcelona), Directora of Investigations Environmental Education
Nereida Parada, University of the Andes, Coordinadora of the Maestría Development Regional Trujillo
Mentioning Adriani, University of the Andes, Maestría in Development Regional
Fernando Aponte, University of the Andes, Maestría in Development Regional
White Araujo, University of the Andes, Maestría in Development Regional
Leonardo Arguello, University of the Andes, Maestría in Development Regional
Lourdes Arrioja, University of the Andes, Maestría in Development Regional
Marineila Butrón, University of the Andes, Maestría in Development Regional
Jesús Caldera, University of the Andes, Maestría in Development Regional
To Cease Calderón, University of the Andes, Maestría in Development Regional
Ninmar Colina, University of the Andes, Maestría in Development Regional
Nancy Escalona, University of the Andes, Maestría in Development Regional
Oswaldo Espinoza, University of the Andes, Maestría in Development Regional
María Hernández, University of the Andes, Maestría in Development Regional
José Gregorio Mendoza, University of the Andes, Maestría in Development Regional
Jorge Milanes, University of the Andes, Maestría in Development Regional
Heber Morales, University of the Andes, Maestría in Development Regional
Darling Perdomo, University of the Andes, Maestría in Development Regional
Yalitza Ramos, University of the Andes, Maestría in Development Regional
Pablo Torres, University of the Andes, Maestría in Development Regional
Doile Valencia, University of the Andes, Maestría in Development Regional
Leticia Viloria, University of the Andes, Maestría in Development Regional
José María Delgado, University of the Llanos, Grupo Environment and Development
Jaime Miró, University of the Llanos, Coordinación Extension
Porfirio Hernández, University of the Llanos, Coordinación Investigation
Tadeo Arismend, University of the Llanos, Coordinación of Postgrado

Foreign Professors

Wolfgang Schuster, University Technical of Cottbus, Coordinador Cottbus
Wolfgang Spyra, University Technical of Cottbus, Faculty of Sciences Environmental
Marie Theres Albert, University Technical of Cottbus, Cátedra of Interculturalidad
Astrid Luedtke, University Technical of Cottbus, Cátedra of Interculturalidad
Peter Ay, University Technical of Cottbus, Faculty of Environmental Sciences
Stephan Simonides, University Technical of Cottbus, Faculty of Environmental Sciences
Isabell Monnerjahn, University Technical of Cottbus, Faculty of Architecture and Ingenieria Civil
Karsten Fritsche, University Technical of Cottbus, Faculty of En- vironmental Sciences
Kai Winkelmann, University Technical of Cottbus, Ingeniero Environmental
Katja Thorwarth, University of Cottbus, Faculty of Architecture
Jörg Walter, University of Cottbus, Faculty of Architecture and Ingenieria Civil
Diethard Mai, University of Gottingen, Director Manager of the Center of Tropical Agriculture—Coordinator GAUG
Gerhard Gerold, University of Gottingen, Departamento of Ecology Regional
Norbert Lanfer, University of Gottingen, Instituto of Geography
Heinrich Pachner, University of Tubingen, Instituto of Geography
Andreas Bohlen, University of Potsdam, Centro of Innovation and Transferencia of Technology
Gerd Paul, University of Frankfurt, Instituto of Social Investigations
Frederick Williams, IC² Institute, University of Texas–Austin, Director, Project Caribe
Victoria Williams, IC² Institute, University of Texas–Austin, Associate Director, Project Caribe
Enrico Fontanari, University of Venecia, Departament of Urbanística

NOTES

1. Available at http://www.ic2.org/Victoria%20Williams-presentation.pdf.
2. In English, *covenants* essentially means "agreements"; or in practice the Spanish term *convenio* is often used internationally.

CHAPTER 19

En Cuba: Biotech, Education, and Health Services

There is no greater paradoxical relation between two nations of the Western Hemisphere than that between the United States of America and La Republica de Cuba, the largest Caribbean nation in geography and population of the West Indies, with exceedingly beautiful beaches, mountains, green slopes, and gentle grasslands, along with well-preserved Spanish colonial architecture and markedly friendly people. Cuba has a major economy (GDP $18.6 billion), which is less than Puerto Rico's ($38.1 billion) or the Dominican Republic's ($50 billion). For comparison, Florida has a gross state product (GSP) of $40 billion. As we discuss in this chapter, there has been a longtime strain in U.S.-Cuba relations. Despite a 10-day threat of nuclear war in the early 1960s and a 40-year U.S. embargo upon trade with Cuba, this country and Cuba should be of maximum strategic interest to another. Relative to the theme of the present book, allow us to introduce the observation that Cuba offers an excellent example of a developing country's use of science and technology to invest in its economy. This latter point, plus the absence of capitalism—for better or worse, depending upon the political values one wishes to call upon—make the Cuban experience among the most captivating reports to ponder in this book.

"HOW WELL YOU DANCE"

People and their cultures are certainly more important than science and technology, so allow us to begin our Cuba discussion with this friendly little story. Several years ago, while attending an economics conference in

Havana, my wife, Victoria, and I (FW) had the good fortune to become acquainted with Anise and Orlando "Cachito" Lopez, the latter the bass player with the internationally popular Cuban music group Buena Vista Social Club. We four very much enjoyed strolling down colorful streets as they showed us Old Havana while exchanging comments about world cities where we had both traveled and about Austin, where the Club was about to travel for a performance.

We agreed it was so unfortunate that Cubans and Americans, being such friendly peoples, and with Florida's Key West being closer to Havana than to Miami, our countries were caught up in an estranged relationship. I explained that it was my government, and not theirs, that required Victoria and me to obtain licenses to visit Cuba. We shared stories about our lives during the missile crisis of October 1962. At that time, Anise described her planning for marriage: "For me and my parents, it was not an easy decision, you understand?" said Anise.

"Were you worried about there maybe being a war?" Victoria responded.

"Heavens, no! I was worried whether a musician would make a stable husband."

Then Orlando summed it up, looking toward Anise and us: "Through revolution and the 40-year embargo, we have survived. Do you know that music isn't on the embargo? It has provided extra money for Anise and me over the years and our link to the outside world; we have lived for and through our music. For you, Anise, through it all, I always have said, 'Que Bueno Baila Usted!'

"For you, Williamses, our Club will play that song in Austin." And two months later, they did.

The Cuban Economic Experience

Historically

During the eighteenth and nineteenth centuries, Cuba was an agrarian nation. Owners of large plantations grew sugar cane, importing slaves from Africa to provide cheap labor—and today, most of Cuba is mixed race, a source of national pride. Mining also began to develop as an industry in this period, including for nickel, chromium, iron, cobalt, copper, and manganese. Additionally, the history of manufacturing in Cuba is mostly one of building sugar mills, some of which were improved in the period of Soviet economic partnership—characterized as a sugar-for-technology transfer. As of this writing, most of these mills are out of date, and there is a controversy about taking them out of commission. The Cuban cigar industry is famous, but it is labor-intensive and not technological as of yet, nor should it be.

Tourism

Tourism developed in the twentieth century, including a rail and ferry link from the U.S. East Coast down the Florida Keys (Flagler Railway) to departure by sea ferry from Key West and across the Florida Straits to Havana. As a major source of income, tourism combined with gambling and associated crime grew in Havana, the latter allegedly overlooked or supported by dictator Fulgencio Batista y Zaldivar.

Tourism can be a fickle industry, prone to change with economic times and in the last several years with terrorism and fear of flying or traveling. We say more later because Cuba has succeeded in the central planning to increase tourism in order to raise funds for development in science and technology.

Revolution

In 1959, a young Cuban attorney, Fidel Castro, led a small revolutionary army out of exile in the Sierra Maestra mountains to overthrow Batista, who immediately fled the country. This had been a mission for Castro, a law graduate of the University of Havana, since 1952, when, as an attorney, he was running for a seat in the Cuban House of Representatives, and Batista halted the election to declare himself president. Castro attempted a revolution in 1953, but failed and fled into the mountains.

Communist Cuba

In 1959, Castro's intentions of founding a communist government were not clear to the United States, which at first had stood aside in the conflict. By 1960, Castro was entering into an economic pact with the Soviet Union and expropriating U.S. and British businesses in his country, all as a part of creating a communist government while also reducing American influence. At this time, the United States severed diplomatic relations while imposing an economic embargo that banned all exports to Cuba, save for a few exceptions. Directly affected was any type of scientific or technology transfer, and this continues largely today.[1] That is why maintaining a '59 Chevy, with no importation of parts, has become an icon of defiant Cuba. In April 1961, the U.S. Central Intelligence Agency backed a group of Cuban exiles making a beach invasion at the Bay of Pigs, which failed and, along with continuing Soviet involvement, further complicated U.S.-Cuba relations.

Early Attention on Building the Cuban Economy

Soon after taking control of the country, President Castro personally decided that fledgling Cuban science would be a major target of investment, and from it could come economic development to move beyond a reliance on sugar and tourism, especially using the biosciences. Today, Cuba is a recognized leader in pharmaceutical R&D, so much so that American reactionaries raised a cry in 2002 about Cuban scientists supposedly being able to develop and export weapons of bioterrorism.

Also of great importance in the early developmental period is that Castro initiated massive programs for public education and health care. These have been most successful, so much so that models of them have been followed in other developing countries, sometimes with Cuban assistance.

Missile Crisis

The U.S.-Cuba estrangement continued in the early 1960s, eventually leading to a crisis when U.S. intelligence found that the Soviets were installing missile systems on the island. In the Cuban Missile Crisis of fall 1962, the Soviet Union and America faced an armed confrontation when the latter demanded that Soviet ships carrying missiles turn around as they steamed toward Cuba. For 10 days in October, the world lay on the brink of nuclear war, and Cuba was in the middle of it. The crisis settled when Soviet ships turned back; the rumor was that Soviet premier Khrushchev negotiated a "no-Cuba" invasion commitment from U.S. president John F. Kennedy.[2]

Cuba Today[3]

The Economy

Table 19.1 summarizes statistics from *The World Factbook* 2001 for Cuba. One can find reasonable corroboration on Cuban data from other publications, like the *Economist*.

Cuban statistics are impressive in education and health care. All Cuban children have access to free public education beginning in kindergarten, including a major summer camp program. President Castro recently completed a restoration and construction program involving 800 schools, which is reaching a goal of having no more than 20 students in a single classroom. The University of Havana (Universidad de la Habana) is a world-class higher education and research resource of the region.[4] It offers a full range of undergraduate and postgraduate programs and hosts or cooperates with various well-known research centers, including in biotechnology. Cuba's Latin American School of Medicine has educated a sufficient number of physicians so that the country now has approximately 60 doctors per 10,000 citizens and, as of this writing, had over 5,000 doctors working abroad, including with a major AIDS program for Africa. The school has recently begun to offer a six-year medical degree program where students, rather than spending a traditional four years in an undergraduate major and then attending medical school for four more years, began studying medicine in their first year.

Table 19.1
Cuba Statistics

DEMOGRAPHY

Population estimate	11,184,023
Infant mortality	7.39/1,000
Life expectancy	76.41 years
Literacy	95.7%
Ethnicity	below*
*mulatto	51%
*white	37%
*black	11%
*Chinese	1%

ECONOMY

GDP (2000 estimate)	$19.2 billion
GDP per capita	$1,700
Labor Force	4.3 million
in agriculture	25%
in industry	24%
in services	51%

LAND USE (1993)

Arable	24%
Permanent crops	7%
Pastures	27%
Forests	24%
Other	18%

Status of Cuban Communism

At the risk of oversimplification, what can or should be said about the consequences of being a communist state in a world where traditional bastions of communism, such as the former Soviet Union and China, have faced radical change? Cuba has survived if not progressed very much economically over the past 40 years. However, their 2000 GDP per capita

($1,700) lags far behind the average ($5,836) of Caribbean nations. This prompts attention to the challenge that if a communist government is to share the wealth, they have to improve their capability for creating it. Given the success of their educational programs, Cuba's human-resource base is a positive factor for economic modernization. But there is also the political side: how can development be kept in conjunction with communist government structure and operation? Without going into detail here, the illegal out-migration of Cubans says much about a lack of balance between social security and personal freedom. Statistics for 2000 show that over 3,000 Cubans attempted to cross the Straits of Florida, of which about 35 percent were interdicted by the U.S. Coast Guard; another estimated 2,400 entered the United States by clandestine flights and overland routes through Mexico.

It is an oversimplification—yes—but Cuban leadership, whether by Dr. Castro or others, faces the challenge of promoting economic growth while maintaining their balance in the delivery of highly regarded education and health services. What's next? Among the very important strengths President Castro has fashioned for his country is to attract many able individuals into positions of leadership. One of these leaders, Speaker of the Cuban House of Representatives Ricardo Alacron, in responding to my (FW) question at a business-development summit held in Cancun about whether they felt threatened that Cuba would be ravaged by abrupt political change such as happened to the divided Germany, was feared in Korea, or was being experienced by the former Soviet Union, gave this answer to our international group of some 200. From my personal notes, I will take the liberty to paraphrase his remarks:

We have developed strong institutions and leadership from the revolution. Our revolution has succeeded despite such challenges as the missile crisis, the American-sponsored Bay of Pigs invasion, the loss of Russia as an economic partner, some of the worst hurricanes of our modern history, crop failures, the fall of world sugar prices, and a 40-year strangling of trade and loss of access to technology by the embargo of our powerful neighbor to the north. From meeting these challenges, we are now experienced, strong, and prepared for whatever is to come our way. Science and technology have been a strength for us; Cuba is open for your business!

The Lesson from Cuba

Although the political debate as well as related criticisms of communist economics could go on and on here, suffice it to say that Cuba has well demonstrated that science and technology can be a part of an economic-development strategy that does not require changing your politics. The able Cubans have shown how targeted economic development, drawing from science and technology, from tourism, or even from sugar, can bring rewarding developmental know-how from the midst of great challenge.

NOTES

1. Embargo administration, as with all of this country's economic sanctions, is handled by the U.S. Treasury Office of Foreign Assets Control (OFAC). See http://www.treas.gov/ for more details and updates.

2. In the years after 1962, work as dean of the Annenberg School at the University of Southern California brought me (FW) into regular contact with Dr. Dean Rusk, former president of the Ford Foundation and secretary of state to John F. Kennedy during the missile crisis. I am sure the late Dr. Rusk would not mind my colleagues and I saying how at a dinner party with him in the 1970s, we were moved by his firsthand description of the absolute chaos of the Cuban Missile Crisis and how young President Kennedy, resisting the pressure of hawks in the government, and with help from his brother, Attorney General Robert Kennedy, managed to avoid what surely would have led to a nuclear confrontation.

3. Cuba has excellent sites on the World Wide Web. A digital version of the daily national newspaper *Granma* is available at http://www.granma.cu/.

4. One can stay abreast of their facilities and activities by consulting their excellent Web site at http://www.uh.cu/.

PART V

Prosperity Sharing

CHAPTER 20

Toward Capitalism with Conscience

One might expect that a book on economic development would have included early on a formal, weighty definition of capitalism. We have not thought this necessary because its definitions in most document contexts or dictionaries are typically straightforward, usually referring to private ownership and a free market. Noteworthy, however, are the critical connotations so often found, and there is no shortage of titles on the topic, as, for example, the over 3,000 books listed by the U.S. Library of Congress with *capitalism* in their title, subtitle, or description. And from today's popular knowledge resource, the World Wide Web, entry of *capitalism* as a search term yields a very wide range of sites ranging from political-science treatises and diatribes to a "Planetary Carnival against Capitalism" held annually in London. Since our book is meant to be transparently procapitalistic, we thought it appropriate to conclude with a chapter addressing the alleged inequities. Can we have capitalism with a conscience? Or perhaps, put another way: can, or how can, there be a capitalism with an emphasis upon quality-of-life components?

MIND-SETS ON CAPITALISM

Not only do attitudes about capitalism diverge greatly, as in the writings of theorists ranging from Karl Marx to modern American economists Milton Friedman or John Kenneth Galbraith, but they likely vary widely in the minds of everyday citizens. Several decades ago George Kozmetsky and several colleagues surveyed over a thousand Americans on their attitudes toward and perceptions of capitalism. The results showed that 23

percent of citizen respondents had no ready definition. Of those who offered one, 47 percent considered private ownership and free market, as
mentioned above, which we considered as "correct," whereas 38 percent
offered responses ranging across such attitude-laden perceptions as "restriction of rights/limited freedom" and "bureaucracy/excessive government." To say the least, then, definitions of capitalism may vary
considerably among everyday citizens, as they do even among specialists
in the world's largest capitalist country.

CONTRAST OF ECONOMIZING AND SOCIALIZING ECONOMIC SYSTEMS

In his landmark treatise *The Coming of Post-Industrial Society,*[1] Daniel Bell
contrasts the design of economic systems where the objective is maximiz-
ing economic returns per se against setting social goals in terms of human
opportunities, as could be specifically defined in terms of access to a desired quality of life, including services for education, health, and financial
benefits to insure a given standard of living. He advocates the requirement
for a complementary balance between the two. A primary focus upon the
human side will fail if we do not give attention to the means for creating
wealth. In the most practical of terms: "If you cannot create the wealth,
then there is nothing to share."

Realizing the risk of oversimplification, for the purposes of discussion
we will consider the "conscience" of capitalism as that of avoiding or
rectifying inequities in the sharing of wealth or prosperity.

CAPITALISM AND FREEDOM

In his widely acclaimed collection of essays published under the above
title, Milton Friedman, 1976 Nobel laureate in economics, makes 12 en-
during examinations regarding aspects of what he calls *competitive capitalism.*[2] They support his main position of the inextricable relation between
capitalism and freedom, including the responsibilities it creates. We summarize these topics below in our own words to provide a consistent style
for this presentation, with a warning and apology if there occur any un-
intentional misinterpretations:[3]

1. There is a dynamic relation between economic and political freedom.
2. The role of government in a free society is chiefly to protect and encourage
   the institutions supporting the democracy, save for activities specifically requiring a national endeavor—for example, national defense.
3. A key socioeconomic goal is the maintenance of stability through monetary
   and budgetary policy contributing to opportunities for citizens, institutions,
   and the free society as a whole.

4. Economic stability requires attention to international financial and trade agreements favorable to the nation's system of free enterprise.

5. The national fiscal policy must recognize the consequences of varying government taxation and expenditures upon the economy and the consequences, pro or con, of employing these for an economic "balance wheel."

6. The operation of a democratic society requires education for the citizenship.

7. History has shown a correlation between the growth of capitalism and the reduction of discrimination involving certain religious or cultural groups.

8. Monopolies possible under free enterprise raise social responsibilities on the parts of business, labor, and government.

9. We must understand and adapt to the dual negative and positive consequences of options for occupational licensure.

10. The key sources of inequities in the distribution of income need identification and remediation.

11. Relative to the foregoing is the necessary attention given to the alternatives and consequences of the various social welfare interventions.

12. How do we conceptualize the alleviation of poverty as a component within a free enterprise economy?

Nowhere has the interdependence of free enterprise and freedom been better articulated than in *Capitalism and Freedom*.

QUALITY OF LIFE

If one is to conceive of a conscience for capitalism, it should be directly measurable by well-known concepts of quality of life. The list below presents commonly acknowledged quality-of-life measures.

The poverty line is also a common concept, referring to a level of income and benefits beneath which one could be considered unable to live at a reasonable level of community standards for basic resources such as food; shelter; and various occupational, health, and educational services. Needless to say, the conscience of any economic system surely reflects upon opportunities to be above the poverty line.

Quality of Life Measures

Healthy environment

Social welfare, benefits, "safety net"

Recreational amenities

Educational opportunities

Health care

Living wage

Opportunity for job enhancement

Affordable housing

Cost of living

Job value

Lifestyle

Transportation

Security, low crime

Cultural programs, experiences

NOTES

1. Daniel Bell, *The Coming of Post-Industrial Society* (New York: Basic Books, 1976).

2. Milton Friedman, *Capitalism and Freedom* (Chicago: University of Chicago Press, 1982).

3. Those who have *Capitalism and Freedom* to consult can note that our items follow the order of chapter topics.

Afterglow: For a Special Tribute

"Afterglow" is a well-known tradition with Kozmetsky-led events, often following an IC² fellows meeting, conferences, or a presentation by a distinguished guest. Whether or not associated with after-dinner liqueurs or music, essentially afterglow is a sharing of warm, professional feelings among all those involved, as if to remind ourselves that there is more to science, technology, and economics than numbers and reports. After all, we are people dealing with people and, most important, with quality of lives.

In the 1980s, when I was very new to the institute and was thinking that "Afterglow" on our conference agenda that time in San Francisco meant Dambuie would be served, Dr. Kozmetsky arose to thank our some 300 representatives of business, government, and academia for spending three days examining the ins and outs of technological wealth and shared prosperity, especially the latter, and the concept of freedom and democracy as essential to human opportunity. He cited himself and his family as an example, recalling how his parents came from Russia with no resources except their new opportunities and ambition to succeed under freedom. He thanked Thomas Jefferson, our third president, for his elegant vision of citizenship and for establishing our public school system. Without it, he explained, he never would have started the education his left-behind relatives never experienced. He would not have gone on through to eventually earn a Harvard degree, become the cofounder of one of America's technological corporations (Teledyne), been able as dean to put the University of Texas College of Business Administration on the map, establish the IC² Institute, or stand this night in San Francisco to be heard and honored by admired friends and esteemed colleagues on a subject he loved and contributed to so intensely. "We live in an America of freedom, abundance, and opportunity. Thank you all."

As we complete *New Wealth*, I take the privilege of adding the last line: *George, you are not only a great American, but what America is all about.*

That's my afterglow for this one. Yes, thank you, sir, from all of us whose lives you've touched.

Frederick Williams

Appendix: Glossary

European Union (EU): An organization of 15 western European countries that promotes cooperation among its members. See http://europa.eu.int/abc-en.htm.

Fast Company: Our concept of a firm, often specializing in technology commercialization, where ever-changing technologies and their markets not only require an especially rapid response capability but anticipation as well. To achieve their necessary pace, these companies require sophisticated uses of information and telecommunication technologies and the know-how to manage innovatively with them. As geared to customer satisfaction, a fast company may strive to operate in the new *Zero Time*.

International Monetary Fund (IMF): An organization that provides short-term credit to its more than 175 member nations. The IMF works to maintain orderly payment arrangements between countries and to promote growth of the world economy without inflation. It supports free trade in goods and services. To stabilize its members' economies, the IMF provides policy advice and short-term loans when a member nation encounters financial difficulty.

To receive IMF loans, members usually must change their economic policies. For example, the IMF may insist that the borrowing country reduce its budget deficit and sharply raise interest rates to reduce inflation. It may also suggest that a member devalue its currency to make its exports more competitive in world markets.

Policies required by the IMF often cause short-term political unrest or economic hardship within the country that adopts them. However, these policies offer important longer-term benefits. They generally stabilize the nation's economy, reduce inflation, and eventually create an economic environment favorable to growth.

By lending money to a member, the IMF reassures private banks and investors that it is safe for them to put money in the country. IMF loans often encourage the extension of existing bank loans and other private credits.

Plans for the IMF were made at the Bretton Woods Conference in 1944. The IMF began operating in 1947. The United States contributed about a third of the new organization's assets. In 1969, the IMF created a type of money called *special drawing rights* (SDRs) to supplement reserves of gold and currency. IMF members can transfer SDRs among themselves to settle debts.

Officially, the IMF is a specialized agency of the United Nations. But in practice, the United States, the United Kingdom, Germany, France, Japan, and Saudi Arabia govern the fund. In its early years, the IMF acted as a meeting place for the industrial nations to discuss their trade relationships and financial dealings with one another. In the 1970s, the fund began focusing on the problems of less developed nations. In the 1990s, the focus shifted toward financial crises in such nations as Indonesia, Mexico, South Korea, and Thailand and in former communist countries such as Russia and Ukraine.

The fund is closely connected with the World Bank, the international agency that offers long-term credit to its member nations. A country must be a member of the IMF before it can belong to the World Bank. The IMF has headquarters in Washington, D.C.

MOU: Memo of Understanding—often an informal document describing agreed areas of cooperation, then used to guide future cooperative projects. Not typically a binding legal document.

RFP: Request for Proposal—outlines tasks or service to be performed, likely funding, and instructions for making an application proposal.

World Bank: An international organization that provides loans to governments and private firms for development projects, such as irrigation, education, and housing. It also grants loans to support government policies that it believes will strengthen a country's economy, such as lower import tariffs and more efficient judicial systems. The bank's official name is the International Bank for Reconstruction and Development. Almost all countries are members of the World Bank. The bank gets most of its funds by borrowing in world financial markets. Its bonds are backed by the pledges of its members and by the loans it makes to governments and firms. The bank is an agency of the United

Nations. Its headquarters are in Washington, D.C. Plans for the World Bank were drawn up at an economic conference held in Bretton Woods, New Hampshire, in 1944. The bank began operating in 1946.

Zero Time: A proprietary management model developed by Professor Raymond Yeh and associates (Yeh, Pearlson, and Kozmetsky; see bibliography) stressing the critical success factors of competing for customer satisfaction in the digital age.

Select Bibliography

Following are publications deemed most relevant to the present work; the list is not meant to cover an entire field or area of subject matter.

Aristide, Jean-Bertrand. *Eyes of the Heart: Seeking a Path for the Poor in the Age of Globalization*. Monroe, Maine: Common Courage Press, 2000.

Barabasi, Albert-Laszlo. *Linked: The New Science of Networks*. Cambridge, Mass.: Perseus Publishing, 2002.

Bell, Daniel. *The Coming of Post-Industrial Society*. New York: Basic Books, 1976.

Castro, Fidel. *Capitalism in Crisis: Globalization and World Politics Today* (with David Deutschmann). La Habana: Ocean Press, 2002.

———. *Capitalismo Actual: Caracterusticas y Contradictions*. La Habana, Cuba: Ocean Press, 1999.

———. *Che: A Memoir*. (with David Deutschmann). La Habana: Ocean Press, 1994.

Castro, Fidel and Alexandra Keeble, *War, Racism, and Economic Justice: The Global Ravages of Capitalism*. La Habana: Ocean Press, 2002.

Clemen, Robert T., and Terence Reilly. *Making Hard Decisions with Decision Tools*. Pacific Grove, Calif.: Brooks/Cole, 2001.

Cooper, William, Stein Thore, David Gibson, and Fred Phillips, eds. *Impact: How IC² Institute Research Affects Public Policy and Business Practices*. Westport, Conn.: Quorum Books, 1997.

Decision Support Software. *Logical Decisions for Windows 95*. Golden, Colo.: Logical Decisions, 1999.

Dordick, Herbert S., and Frederick Williams. *Innovative Management Using Telecommunications*. New York: Wiley, 1986.

Friedman, Milton. *Capitalism and Freedom*. Chicago: University of Chicago Press, 1982.

Friedman, Thomas L. *Longitudes and Attitudes: The Other Side of Globalism.* New York: Farrar, Straus & Giroux, 2002.

Kozmetsky, George, and Raymond W. Smilor, eds. *The Technopolis Phenomenon.* Austin, Tex.: IC² Institute, 1990.

Monge, Peter R., and Noshir S. Contractor. *Theories of Communication Networks.* Oxford: Oxford University Press, 2004.

Schuyler, John. *Risk and Decision Analysis in Projects.* 2nd ed. Newton Square, Pa.: Project Management Institute, 2001.

Stiglitz, Joseph E., *Globalization and Its Discontents.* New York: W. W. Norton, 2002.

Williams, Frederick. *The New Telecommunications.* New York: Free Press, 1991.

Williams, Frederick, and Herbert S. Dordick. *The Executive's Guide to Information Technology.* New York: Wiley, 1983.

Williams, Frederick, and David V. Gibson, eds. *Technology Transfer: A Communications Perspective.* Newbury Park, Calif.: Sage, 1990.

Williams, Frederick, and Peter Monge. *Reasoning with Statistics.* 5th ed. Fort Worth, Texas: Harcourt College Publishers, 2001.

Wilson, Samuel, ed. *The Indigenous People of the Caribbean.* Miami: Florida Anthropological Association, 1998.

Yeh, Raymond, Keri Pearlson, and George Kozmetsky. *Zero Time: Providing Instant Customer Value—Every Time, All the Time.* New York: Wiley, 2000.

Index

About the Authors

GEORGE KOZMETSKY was cofounder of the Teledyne Corporation, former dean of the University of Texas College of Business, and founder and chairman of the University of Texas IC^2 Institute. At the University of Texas at Austin, Dr. Kozmetsky was also Murray S. Walker Chair Professor and E. D. Walker Centennial Fellow. On September 30, 1993, Dr. Kozmetsky received the National Medal of Technology from President Bill Clinton. He was the author or editor of many books and articles, including *Modern American Capitalism* and *Immigrant and Minority Entrepreneurship*, and in 2003, he took the lead in launching Project CBIRD, a binational initiative promoting economic development along the U.S.-Mexico border. On April 30, 2003, George Kozmetsky died at age 85 after a long illness.

FREDERICK WILLIAMS, a social scientist specializing in the economics of information technologies, was founding dean of the Annenberg School for Communication at the University of Southern California. At the University of Texas, he has occupied the Mary Gibbs Jones Chair in Communications and serves as the W. W. Heath Centennial Fellow in the University's IC^2 Institute. Among his books are *The New Urban Infrastructure* and *Telecommunications Policy and Economic Development*.

VICTORIA WILLIAMS is executive director of the Williams Group, providing consulting services in education and economic development. As codirector of the IC^2 Institute's Project Caribe at the University of Texas at Austin, she has been involved with economic-development work in the

Caribbean basin. Her current work concerns Cuba's transition to capitalism. Her experience includes serving as superintendent of schools in Texas
and New Jersey. She is author of numerous articles on the relationship
between education and economic development, and the research report
Technopolis Construction in the Caribbean.